Cooking Light

Everyday
Baking

Softcover ISBN-13: 978-0-8487-3441-1
Softcover ISBN-10: 0-8487-3441-6
Hardcover ISBN-13: 978-0-8487-3518-0
Hardcover ISBN-10: 0-8487-3518-8
Library of Congress Control Number: 2011941430

Printed in the United States of America
First printing 2012

Be sure to check with your health-care provider before making any changes in your diet.

Oxmoor House

VP, Publishing Director: Jim Childs
Editorial Director: Leah McLaughlin
Creative Director: Felicity Keane
Brand Manager: Michelle Turner Aycock
Senior Editor: Heather Averett
Managing Editor: Rebecca Benton

Cooking Light® Everyday Baking

Editor: Rachel Quinlivan West, RD
Project Editor: Sarah H. Doss
Senior Designer: Emily Albright Parrish
Assistant Designer: Allison Sperando Potter
Director, Test Kitchen: Elizabeth Tyler Austin
Assistant Directors, Test Kitchen: Julie Christopher, Julie Gunter
Recipe Developers and Testers: Wendy Ball, RD; Victoria E. Cox; Stefanie Maloney; Callie Nash; Leah Van Deren
Recipe Editor: Alyson Moreland Haynes
Food Stylists: Margaret Monroe Dickey, Catherine Crowell Steele
Photography Director: Jim Bathie
Senior Photo Stylist: Kay E. Clarke
Photo Stylist: Katherine Eckert Coyne
Assistant Photo Stylist: Mary Louise Menendez
Senior Production Manager: Greg A. Amason

Contributors

Copy Editors: Norma Butterworth-McKittrick, Jacqueline Giovanelli
Proofreader: Dolores Hydock
Indexer: Mary Ann Laurens
Interns: Erin Bishop, Christine T. Boatwright, Mackenzie Cogle, Georgia Dodge, Laura Hoxworth, Susan Kemp, Emily Robinson
Recipe Developers and Testers: Elizabeth Nelson, Kathleen Royal Phillips
Photographers: Jennifer Davick, Mary Britton Senseney
Photo Stylists: Missie Neville Crawford, Mindi Shapiro Levine, Lydia DeGaris Pursell, Leslie Simpson
Food Stylist: Marian Cooper Cairns

Time Home Entertainment Inc.

Publisher: Richard Fraiman
Vice President, Strategy & Business Development: Steven Sandonato
Executive Director, Marketing Services: Carol Pittard
Executive Director, Retail & Special Sales: Tom Mifsud
Director, Bookazine Development & Marketing: Laura Adam
Executive Publishing Director: Joy Butts
Finance Director: Glenn Buonocore
Associate General Counsel: Helen Wan

Cooking Light®

Editor: Scott Mowbray
Creative Director: Carla Frank
Executive Managing Editor: Phillip Rhodes
Executive Editor, Food: Ann Taylor Pittman
Special Publications Editor: Mary Simpson Creel, MS, RD
Senior Food Editors: Timothy Q. Cebula, Julianna Grimes
Senior Editor: Cindy Hatcher
Assistant Editor, Nutrition: Sidney Fry, MS, RD
Assistant Editors: Kimberly Holland, Phoebe Wu
Test Kitchen Director: Vanessa T. Pruett
Assistant Test Kitchen Director: Tiffany Vickers Davis
Recipe Testers and Developers: Robin Bashinsky, Adam Hickman, Deb Wise
Art Directors: Fernande Bondarenko, Shawna Kalish
Associate Art Director: Rachel Cardina Lasserre
Designers: Hagen Stegall, Dréa Zacharenko
Assistant Designer: Nicole Gerrity
Photo Director: Kristen Schaefer
Assistant Photo Editor: Amy Delaune
Senior Photographer: Randy Mayor
Senior Photo Stylist: Cindy Barr
Photo Stylist: Leigh Ann Ross
Chief Food Stylist: Charlotte Autry
Senior Food Stylist: Kellie Gerber Kelley
Food Styling Assistant: Blakeslee Wright
Production Director: Liz Rhoades
Production Editor: Hazel R. Eddins
Assistant Production Editor: Josh Rutledge
Copy Chief: Maria Parker Hopkins
Assistant Copy Chief: Susan Roberts
Research Editor: Michelle Gibson Daniels
Administrative Coordinator: Carol D. Johnson
Cookinglight.com Editor: Allison Long Lowery
Nutrition Editor: Holley Johnson Grainger, MS, RD
Associate Editor/Producer: Mallory Daugherty Brasseale

To order additional publications, call 1-800-765-6400 or 1-800-491-0551.

For more books to enrich your life, **visit oxmoorhouse.com**

To search, savor, and share thousands of recipes, visit **myrecipes.com**

Contents

Welcome

Baking is one of those kitchen tasks that is at the root of lovely memories, whether making something delicious with your grandmother or stealing tastes of cookie dough while your mom or dad wasn't looking (or so you thought). Baking is an opportunity to connect and savor the delights of the kitchen.

Those moments don't have to be reserved for weekends or holidays when you have extra time. They can in fact be a part of every day, which is the purpose of *Cooking Light Everyday Baking*. It was created for readers like you who want to bake, but need quick, healthy options that don't require spending too much time in the kitchen. It provides an array of favorite recipes that are suitable for the whole family, and the best part is that each recipe requires 30 minutes or less of hands-on prep time so you can keep your time in the kitchen to a minimum. We hope this book opens up more of your days to the pleasures of baking.

—the editors of *Cooking Light*

Getting Started

Getting Started

With a few pieces of equipment and some basic ingredients, you can prepare delicious, healthy baked goods every day. Here are tips to get you started and to ensure baking success.

1. Know your oven. It's important to know how your oven operates. Many ovens, including new, expensive models, may run hotter or colder than the temperature you want, and many ovens change as they age. Keep an oven thermometer in your oven so you always know the temperature.

You also need to be aware of hot spots, which can cause uneven cake layers or a few overly browned cookies in each batch. Try the bread test: Arrange bread slices in a single layer on a baking sheet. Bake at 350° for a few minutes to see which pieces, if any, become darker than others. If some do, you've found your hot spots and can avoid those areas or rotate pans to compensate.

2. Preheat. Although it's tempting, don't put your baked goods in the oven before it's preheated. If the oven has not reached the correct temperature, your recipe will take longer to bake and you run the risk of having a dry texture and low volume.

Once your baked goods are in the oven, keep the oven door closed tightly; the temperature fluctuates each time the door opens, and these fluctuations can lead to a variety of problems. If the oven temperature drops, the baked product will probably bake a bit more slowly, and it may sink in the center, depending on what you're baking. Then, as the oven reheats to the required temperature, the edges will be exposed to more extreme temperatures, which could possibly result in a dry, tough final product.

3. Begin with ingredients at approximately room temperature (65° to 70°). Simply leave eggs, butter, milk, and any other refrigerated items out on the kitchen counter for about 30 minutes while you measure and gather the remaining ingredients and equipment. Room-temperature ingredients blend together more easily and room-temperature egg whites beat to maximum volume.

4. Measure carefully. Baking, particularly light baking, is a science that requires precise measurements. So, unlike other dishes where a little less or a little more of an ingredient won't really matter, in light baking, even an extra tablespoon of flour can change the texture of a reduced-fat cake. To get the best results, follow the directions precisely.

5. Choose the proper pan size and color. Use the pan size the recipe calls for. A too-small pan could cause overflow, while a too-large pan may leave your cake flatter than you wanted. The color of the pan matters, too. Choose aluminum pans with a dull finish since metal absorbs and conducts heat evenly. Avoid shiny pans, which deflect heat, and dark metal pans, which can cause baked goods to brown too quickly before the inside is done. If you must substitute glass or ceramic baking dishes for dark metal baking pans, decrease the oven temperature by 25 degrees, and check early for doneness.

An Everyday Baker's
Pantry List

Flour: These recipes call for a variety of flours, and it's important to use the flour specified. Here's why: Many different flours are available that contain varying levels of protein, which form gluten that gives baked goods elasticity and structure—the more protein, the more gluten. The amount of gluten you need depends on what you're baking, and too much or too little can adversely affect the texture. Bread flour has the most protein and produces denser items; cake flour has the least, yielding very light baked goods; and all-purpose is a middle-of-the-road flour in terms of protein and creates tender cakes.

Sugar: Sugar has three critical functions in baking: It slows gluten development, keeping the texture tender; it absorbs liquid, maintaining moisture; and it caramelizes during baking, adding flavor. In addition to common white granulated sugar, several other sugars appear in these recipes. Some, like brown sugar, are added to the batter or dough; others, such as turbinado, are sprinkled over the top of a baked good to provide texture and crunch.

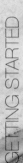

GETTING STARTED

Fats: Fats, like butter, oil, or shortening, coat the flour proteins, slow gluten formation, and provide moisture, which ensures tenderness. We use butter, not butter substitutes. It provides richness and carries the flavor of other ingredients. If a recipe calls for softened butter, the butter should yield slightly to gentle pressure. If it's too soft, cookies may spread or cakes may end up dense. Let butter soften at room temperature for about 30 minutes. Avoid using the microwave as it's too easy to melt the butter rather than soften it.

Salt: Salt is indispensible in baking. It enhances and rounds out the flavor of almost every ingredient it touches, even sweets. Salt brightens flavors, balances the bitterness of certain foods, acts as a preservative, and tenderizes. Without it, many baked goods would taste flat and dull. We use it judiciously in our recipes to ensure the sodium levels remain reasonable.

Eggs: The two parts of an egg—the white and the yolk—react differently in baked goods. Whites are a drying and leavening agent, while yolks contain fat and lecithin, which allows fats and water to mix smoothly and ensures an even, tender texture.

Milk and buttermilk: Milk contains protein, which gives baked goods structure. Buttermilk (an acidic ingredient) also tenderizes. Lower-fat or fat-free milk or buttermilk is a good option— and used often in these recipes—when the dairy fat doesn't play a crucial role in the texture and flavor of the baked good.

Leaveners: Leavening agents, such as baking powder and baking soda, produce carbon dioxide bubbles, which are trapped by the starch in the batter or dough and expand during baking, causing it to rise.

Vanilla extract: The concentrated flavor of vanilla is a popular addition to baked goods. Though imitation vanilla is less expensive, it doesn't match the rounded and complex flavors found in the genuine pure extract. Imitation vanilla is made from paper manufacturing byproducts treated with chemicals, and its flavor often has a harsh finish.

Cooking spray: In light baking, cooking spray is crucial to prevent baked goods from sticking to pans.

An Everyday Baker's Essential

Equipment

Appliances

Food processor: This appliance will chop, shred, and grate for you. It can also make pastry dough easily and quickly. Be aware, though, that processor bowls will leak at the base if overloaded with liquid. A mini food processor is helpful for small chopping jobs.

Electric mixer: There are two kinds of mixers: a portable handheld mixer for small mixing jobs and a stand mixer (regular or heavy-duty) for substantial baking. Lightweight portable mixers allow you to control the mixer's movement in a freestanding bowl. Heavy-duty stand mixers are more powerful and come with attachments and a large-capacity bowl.

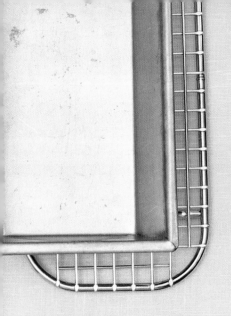

Bakeware

Be sure you always use the pan size specified in a recipe. The correct way to measure pans is across the inside top edges.

Baking pans and dishes: Pans are metal; dishes are glass or ceramic. If a recipe calls for a pan and you have only glass in that size, reduce the oven temperature by 25 degrees and check for doneness earlier. Here are some common baking pans and dishes:

- 8- and 9-inch square pans and baking dishes
- 13 x 9–inch pan and baking dish
- 11 x 7–inch baking dish

Baking sheets: Purchase large, sturdy baking sheets. A 15 x 10–inch jelly-roll pan is also useful.

Loaf pans: Metal pans measuring 9 x 5 inches and 8 x 4 inches are most common.

Muffin pans: Buy a muffin pan that holds 12 muffins, a typical yield for muffin recipes. Most muffin pan cups measure 2½ inches across the top. A mini-muffin pan is handy, too, and gives you the option to go smaller.

Pie plates: For pie plates, use glass, ceramic, or dull metal. The standard size is 9 inches. Deep-dish pie plates are 9½ inches.

Cake pans: Eight and 9-inch round cake pans are helpful pieces of baking equipment. Buy multiples to streamline prep if you bake cakes often. Also, consider a tube pan for angel food cake, a Bundt pan for pound cake, a 9-inch springform pan for cheesecakes, and a tart pan.

Wire racks: Collect two or three large rectangular wire racks for cookie baking. For cake layers, small round and oval racks work well.

Utensils

Bowls: Choose mixing bowls in graduated sizes so you can tailor the size you need to the recipe you're preparing. Plus, they'll be easy to stack and store. Glass, plastic, or earthenware bowls work for most mixing. Stainless steel and glass work best for mixing cake batter.

Cutting boards: A wooden cutting board and a plastic cutting board are essential kitchen tools. It's ideal to have a designated board for cutting fruits and vegetables and another for cutting meats to prevent cross-contamination from raw meats to your fresh produce. Make sure you sanitize your boards regularly.

Grater: The best box grater has four sizes of grating holes. A Microplane is also helpful for small jobs like grating citrus rind, hard cheeses, and chocolate.

Measuring cups: Measuring cups—both dry and liquid—are essential. Liquid measuring cups have a handle and spout and are designed so you can view the contents at eye level to make sure you have the correct amount. Dry measuring cups are flat on top, so you can mound in dry ingredients, like flour and sugar, and level them off for precise measurements.

Measuring spoons: Select a set that graduates from ⅛ teaspoon to 1 tablespoon.

Oven thermometer: Using an oven thermometer will help you make sure your oven is reaching the required temperatures, which is a crucial part of getting the best results in your baked goods.

Pastry blender: This time-saving tool simplifies cutting fat (usually butter) into the flour mixture until it resembles coarse meal. You can use two knives if you like, but it will add time to your prep.

Rolling pin: A large rolling pin is a basic tool that works well for rolling biscuits and cookie dough.

Kitchen scale: Weighing is the most accurate way to measure flour. Depending on how tightly you pack a measuring cup, you could end up with much more flour than intended. A kitchen scale can remedy that.

Strainers: Strainers have a coarse or fine wire mesh and are used to drain or separate liquids from solids and to separate coarse particles from fine ones.

Whisks: Choose elongated stainless-steel wire whisks for blending batters and sauces and a balloon whisk for whipping egg whites. They come in a variety of sizes, but a medium whisk will serve most of your baking needs well.

Rolls &
Flatbreads

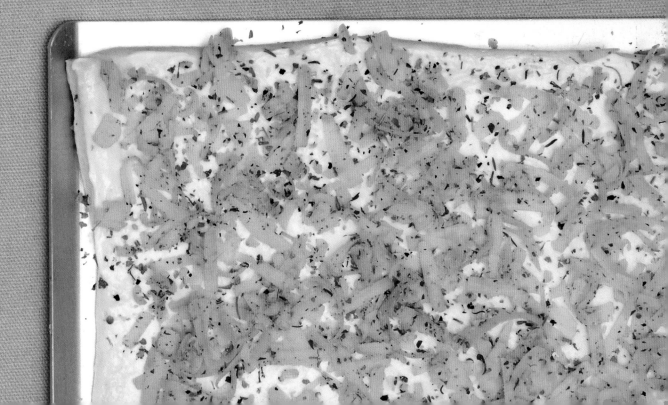

Sour Cream Rolls

8.8 ounces low-fat baking mix (about 2¼ cups), divided	**2 tablespoons canola oil**
1 (8-ounce) carton fat-free sour cream	**2 teaspoons chopped fresh chives**
6 tablespoons butter, melted	**Cooking spray**

1. Preheat oven to 350°. Weigh or lightly spoon baking mix into dry measuring cups; level with a knife. Combine 2 cups baking mix and next 4 ingredients, stirring well.

2. Sprinkle remaining ¼ cup baking mix on work surface. Drop dough by level tablespoons onto surface; roll into 36 balls. Place 3 balls into each of 12 muffin cups coated with cooking spray. Coat dough balls lightly with cooking spray. Bake at 350° for 20 to 25 minutes or until rolls are lightly browned. Serve immediately. **Serves 12 (serving size: 1 roll).**

CALORIES 163; FAT 9.5g (sat 3.8g, mono 3.8g, poly 1.1g); PROTEIN 2.8g; CARB 17g; FIBER 0.5g; CHOL 18mg; IRON 0.8mg; SODIUM 279mg; CALC 141mg

■ BAKING 101 TIP

Baking mix can be helpful for novice bakers. With the leaveners already mixed into the flour and other dry ingredients, you simply have to stir in the wet ingredients (eggs, butter, oil, milk, or sour cream), and bake.

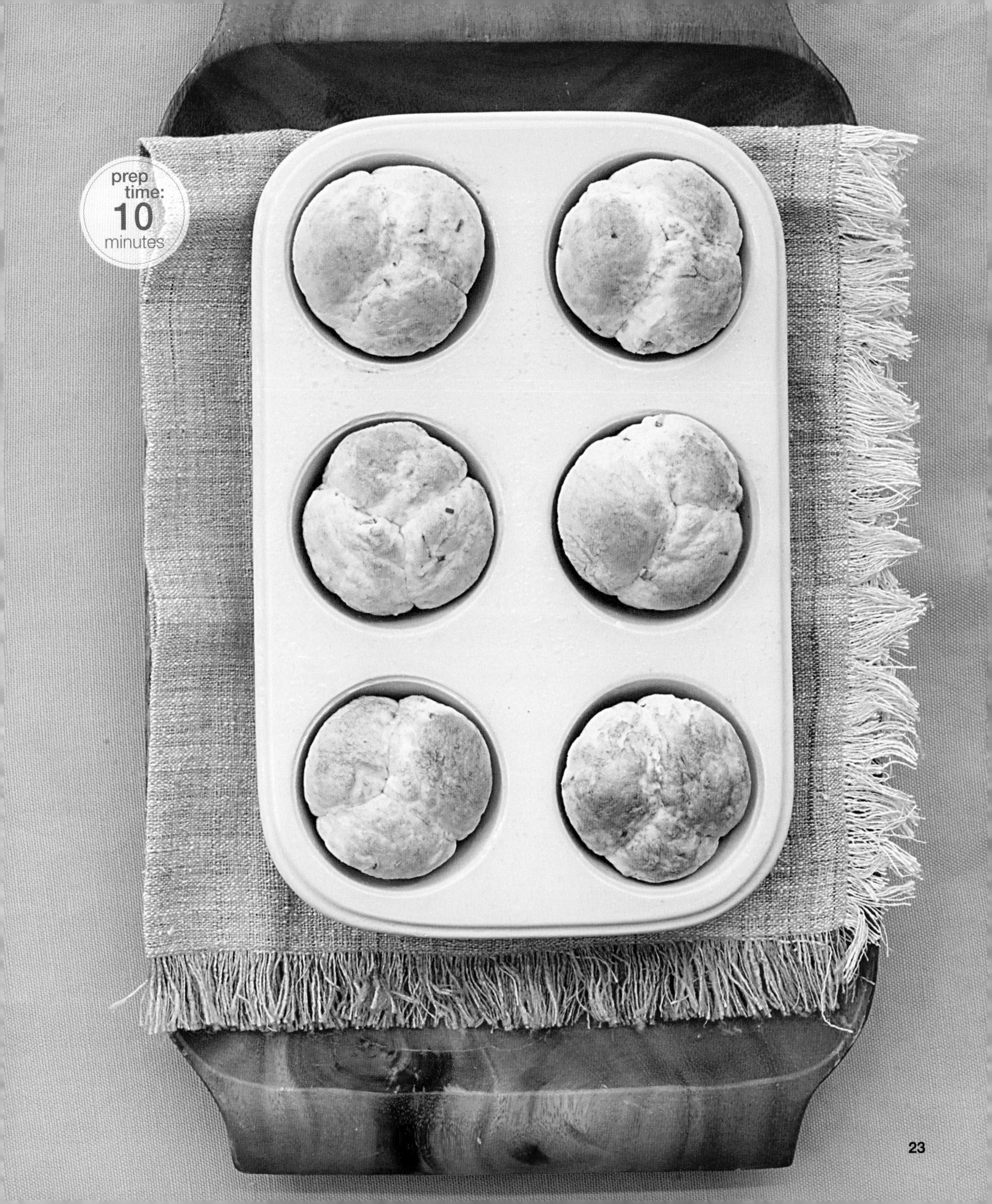

Herbed Passover Rolls

1¼ **cups water**
⅓ **cup canola oil**
1 **tablespoon sugar**
1 **teaspoon kosher salt**

2 **cups matzo meal**
4 **large eggs**
1 **tablespoon chopped fresh chives**
2 **teaspoons finely chopped fresh thyme**

1. Preheat oven to 375°. Cover a large, heavy baking sheet with parchment paper.
2. Combine first 4 ingredients in a medium saucepan over medium-high heat; bring to a boil. Reduce heat to low; add matzo meal, stirring well with a wooden spoon until mixture pulls away from sides of pan (about 30 seconds). Remove from heat; place dough in bowl of a stand mixer. Cool slightly. Add eggs, 1 at a time, beating at low speed with paddle attachment until well combined, and scraping sides and bottom of bowl after each egg addition. Stir in chives and thyme.
3. With moistened fingers, shape about ¼ cupfuls of dough into 12 mounds, and place 2 inches apart onto prepared pan. Bake at 375° for 55 minutes or until browned and crisp. Cool on a wire rack. **Serves 12 (serving size: 1 roll).**

CALORIES 134; FAT 8g (sat 1g, mono 4.3g, poly 2.1g); PROTEIN 3.8g; CARB 12.5g; FIBER 0.6g; CHOL 71mg; IRON 1mg; SODIUM 181mg; CALC 13mg

■ BAKING 101 TIP

Matzo meal is ground matzo, or unleavened
bread, which is used as a substitute for
flour in Passover cooking. It's available in
the kosher or ethnic section of grocery
stores. To make ahead, cool rolls completely,
and freeze for up to one month.

prep
time:
13
minutes

Spotted Puppies

15.75 ounces all-purpose flour (about 3½ cups)
1 teaspoon baking soda
¼ teaspoon salt
½ cup golden raisins

2 teaspoons sugar
1⅔ cups low-fat buttermilk
1 large egg, lightly beaten

1. Preheat oven to 425°. Weigh or lightly spoon flour into dry measuring cups; level with a knife. Combine flour, baking soda, and salt in a large bowl, stirring with a whisk; stir in raisins and sugar. Combine buttermilk and egg; add to flour mixture, stirring until dough forms.

2. Turn dough out onto a lightly floured surface; knead lightly 4 times with floured hands (dough will be sticky). Divide dough into 12 equal portions, shaping each into a ball (cover remaining dough to prevent drying). Arrange rolls on a lightly floured baking sheet. Bake at 425° for 10 minutes. Reduce oven temperature to 400° (do not remove rolls from oven); bake an additional 8 minutes or until rolls sound hollow when tapped. **Serves 12 (serving size: 1 roll).**

CALORIES 178; FAT 1.1g (sat 0.4g, mono 0.3g, poly 0.2g); PROTEIN 5.7g; CARB 36.2g; FIBER 1.3g; CHOL 19mg; IRON 1.9mg; SODIUM 197mg; CALC 51mg

■ BAKING 101 TIP

Spotted Puppies, a variant of Irish soda bread, get their name from the raisins that spot their appearance. The trick when making this bread is not to overmix the dough. Mix and knead it as quickly and gently as possible so the rolls turn out light.

Fresh Thyme Popovers

4.5 ounces all-purpose flour (about 1 cup)
2 teaspoons minced fresh thyme
½ teaspoon salt
1 cup 1% low-fat milk
2 large eggs

1 tablespoon butter, melted
Cooking spray
1 tablespoon finely grated Parmigiano-Reggiano cheese

1. Preheat oven to 375°. Weigh or lightly spoon flour into a dry measuring cup; level with a knife. Combine flour, thyme, and salt, stirring with a whisk. Combine milk and eggs in a medium bowl, stirring with a whisk until blended; let stand 30 minutes. Gradually add flour mixture to milk mixture, stirring well with a whisk. Stir in melted butter.
2. Coat 8 popover cups with cooking spray; sprinkle cheese evenly among cups. Place cups in oven, and bake at 375° for 5 minutes. Divide batter evenly among prepared cups. Bake at 375° for 40 minutes or until golden. Serve immediately. **Serves 8 (serving size: 1 popover).**

CALORIES 97; FAT 2.9g (sat 1.5g, mono 1g, poly 0.3g); PROTEIN 4.3g; CARB 12.4g; FIBER 0.4g; CHOL 51mg; IRON 1mg; SODIUM 200mg; CALC 52mg

prep
time:
9
minutes

■ BAKING 101 TIP

Popover cups are tall and narrow so the batter "pops over" the top as it bakes; you can find a popover pan at any kitchenware shop. Muffin cups will also do (with five minutes less time in the oven), though the rolls won't puff quite as dramatically. Make the popover batter up to two hours ahead, and refrigerate until 15 minutes before you plan to bake them.

Savory Sausage Breakfast Rolls

1 (11-ounce) can refrigerated French bread
   dough
2 tablespoons butter, melted
2 teaspoons chopped fresh sage

8 ounces reduced-fat pork sausage, cooked and
   crumbled
¾ cup (3 ounces) shredded Gruyère cheese
Cooking spray

1. Preheat oven to 350°. Unroll dough into a rectangle on a lightly floured surface. Roll dough into a 13 x 8–inch rectangle; brush with butter, leaving a ½-inch border. Combine sage and sausage. Sprinkle sausage mixture evenly over dough, leaving a ½-inch border; top with cheese. Starting with a long side, roll dough up, jelly-roll fashion; press seam to seal (do not seal ends of roll). Cut 1 (½-inch-thick) crosswise slice from each end; discard. Slice roll crosswise into 12 (1-inch-thick) pieces; arrange in a 13 x 9–inch baking dish coated with cooking spray. Bake at 350° for 28 minutes or until golden. **Serves 12 (serving size: 1 roll).**

CALORIES 156; FAT 8.4g (sat 4g, mono 3.2g, poly 0.6g); PROTEIN 7.8g; CARB 12.4g; FIBER 0g; CHOL 26mg; IRON 0.9mg; SODIUM 323mg; CALC 73mg

■ BAKING 101 TIP

You'll need to leave a ½-inch border around the edge of the dough to make sure the seams will stay sealed when you roll it up. We like reduced-fat pork sausage in this recipe, but turkey sausage also works.

ROLLS & FLATBREADS

Orange Breakfast Rolls

¼ cup finely chopped pecans, toasted
2 teaspoons grated fresh orange rind, divided
2 tablespoons fresh orange juice, divided
1 tablespoon butter, melted

Cooking spray
1 (8-ounce) can refrigerated reduced-fat crescent dinner roll dough
¼ cup sifted powdered sugar

1. Preheat oven to 375°. Combine pecans, 1 teaspoon rind, 1 tablespoon juice, and melted butter in a small bowl.
2. Coat a large baking sheet with cooking spray. Unroll dough on pan, and separate into 2 rectangles, gently pressing seams together with fingertips. Spread orange rind mixture evenly over rectangles. Roll up each rectangle, starting with a short edge, pressing firmly to eliminate air pockets; pinch seam to seal. Using a serrated knife, cut each roll evenly into 8 (1-inch) slices. Place slices on pan. Bake at 375° for 12 minutes or until rolls turn golden brown. Remove rolls from pan, and place on a wire rack over wax paper.
3. While rolls bake, combine remaining 1 teaspoon orange rind, remaining 1 tablespoon orange juice, and powdered sugar in a small bowl, stirring until smooth. Drizzle glaze evenly over warm rolls. **Serves 16 (serving size: 1 roll).**

CALORIES 73; FAT 4.3g (sat 1.6g, mono 1.6g, poly 0.7g); PROTEIN 1.2g; CARB 8.4g; FIBER 0.2g; CHOL 2mg; IRON 0.4mg; SODIUM 117mg; CALC 2mg

■ SHORTCUT TIP
To speed preparation, place pecans on a baking sheet, and toast them in the oven while it preheats.

Lemon-Glazed Sweet Rolls

1 (13.8-ounce) can refrigerated pizza crust
   dough
⅓ cup apple jelly
⅔ cup raisins

Cooking spray
½ cup sifted powdered sugar
1½ teaspoons fresh lemon juice
1 teaspoon hot water

1. Preheat oven to 400°. Unroll pizza dough, and pat dough into a 12 x 9–inch rectangle. Spread jelly over dough, leaving a ½-inch border. Sprinkle raisins over jelly, pressing gently into dough. Beginning with a long side, roll up jelly-roll fashion, and pinch seam to seal (do not seal ends of roll). Cut roll into 12 (1-inch) slices. Place slices, cut sides up, in muffin cups coated with cooking spray. Bake at 400° for 15 minutes or until golden. Remove rolls from pan, and place on a wire rack over wax paper.
2. Combine powdered sugar, lemon juice, and 1 teaspoon hot water in small bowl, stirring until smooth. Drizzle glaze evenly over warm rolls. **Serves 12 (serving size: 1 roll).**

CALORIES 147; FAT 1.1g (sat 0.3g, mono 0g, poly 0.3g); PROTEIN 2.8g; CARB 32.7g; FIBER 0.8g; CHOL 0mg; IRON 1.1mg; SODIUM 237mg; CALC 4mg

■ BAKING 101 TIP
Sifting the powdered sugar helps remove any lumps, creating a smoother glaze.

Cinnamon Buttons

Cooking spray
3 tablespoons unsalted butter, melted and divided
6 tablespoons sugar
¾ teaspoon ground cinnamon
1 (11-ounce) can refrigerated soft breadstick dough

1. Preheat oven to 375°. Lightly coat 6 muffin cups with cooking spray.

2. Pour 2 tablespoons melted butter into a shallow dish. Combine sugar and cinnamon in another shallow dish.

3. Unroll dough; separate into breadsticks. Cut each breadstick into 3 equal portions; shape each portion into a ball. Working with 1 ball at a time, dip into melted butter; gently roll in sugar mixture. Place 6 balls in each muffin cup. Brush remaining 1 tablespoon melted butter evenly over rolls. Bake at 375° for 15 minutes. Remove rolls from pan. Serve warm. **Serves 6 (serving size: 1 roll).**

CALORIES 242; FAT 8.4g (sat 5.2g, mono 2g, poly 0.7g); PROTEIN 4.1g; CARB 37.9g; FIBER 0.9g; CHOL 15mg; IRON 1.5mg; SODIUM 371mg; CALC 5mg

■ SHORTCUT TIP

You can use kitchen shears to easily cut the dough into pieces. Cutting, shaping, dipping, and rolling the dough balls are easy tasks that kids can help with if they'd like. Sprinkle any remaining cinnamon-sugar over the top of the dough before baking.

prep
time:
12
minutes

37

■ BAKING 101 TIP

To pack brown sugar, spoon it into a dry measuring cup, and then press the sugar into the measuring cup with the back of a spoon. Add and pack until it reaches the rim, and then level it with the flat side of a knife.

ROLLS & FLATBREADS

Quick Cranberry Crescent Rolls

¼ cup packed brown sugar
½ teaspoon ground cinnamon
1 (8-ounce) can refrigerated reduced-fat
   crescent dinner roll dough
¼ cup cranberry-orange crushed fruit

2 tablespoons chopped walnuts
Cooking spray
¼ cup sifted powdered sugar
1¼ teaspoons 1% low-fat milk
¼ teaspoon vanilla extract

1. Preheat oven to 375°. Combine brown sugar and cinnamon in a small bowl; set aside.
2. Unroll dough, and separate into 8 triangles. Spread crushed fruit evenly over each triangle. Sprinkle triangles evenly with brown sugar mixture and walnuts. Roll crescents according to package directions, and pinch ends of crescents to seal. Place rolls, point sides down, on a baking sheet coated with cooking spray. Bake at 375° for 13 to 15 minutes or until golden brown.
3. While rolls bake, combine powdered sugar, milk, and vanilla, stirring until smooth. Remove rolls from oven. Remove from pan, and cool slightly on a wire rack over wax paper. Drizzle glaze evenly over warm rolls.
Serves 8 (serving size: 1 roll).

CALORIES 161; FAT 5.9g (sat 2.1g, mono 1.7g, poly 1.4g); PROTEIN 2.3g; CARB 26.7g; FIBER 0.3g; CHOL 0mg; IRON 0.9mg; SODIUM 226mg; CALC 10mg

prep
time:
12
minutes

Lemon-Rosemary Focaccia

1 (8-ounce) can refrigerated reduced-fat crescent dinner roll dough
1 small lemon, cut into paper-thin slices
1 tablespoon fresh rosemary leaves
1 tablespoon pine nuts
¼ teaspoon coarse sea salt
¼ teaspoon cracked black pepper
Olive oil–flavored cooking spray

1. Preheat oven to 375°. Unroll dough onto an ungreased baking sheet, being careful not to separate dough into pieces. Gently press dough together along seams to seal. Arrange lemon slices evenly over dough. Sprinkle evenly with rosemary leaves and next 3 ingredients; lightly coat with cooking spray.

2. Place on bottom rack in oven, and bake at 375° for 14 minutes or until edges are golden. Cut into 8 equal pieces. Serve warm. **Serves 8 (serving size: 1 piece).**

CALORIES 101; FAT 5.4g (sat 2.1g, mono 1.7g, poly 0.9g); PROTEIN 2.2g; CARB 12.9g; FIBER 0.3g; CHOL 0mg; IRON 0.8mg; SODIUM 294mg; CALC 3mg

■ BAKING 101 TIP

Coarse sea salt has a bright, clean taste. It's typically not as refined as other processed salts, so it still contains natural traces of minerals such as iron, magnesium, calcium, potassium, zinc, and iodine that give it subtle nuances of flavor.

Rosemary-Prosciutto Breadsticks

1 (11-ounce) can refrigerated soft breadstick dough
1½ ounces thinly sliced prosciutto, cut into ½-inch strips

Olive oil–flavored cooking spray
3 tablespoons grated Parmesan cheese
2 teaspoons minced fresh rosemary

1. Preheat oven to 375°. Unroll dough, separating into 12 strips; cut each strip in half lengthwise. Wrap prosciutto slices around 12 dough strips. Twist unwrapped dough strips around prosciutto-wrapped pieces; twist 3 to 4 times, pinching ends to seal. Coat breadsticks with cooking spray.

2. Combine cheese and rosemary in a pie plate or shallow dish; roll breadsticks in cheese mixture. Place breadsticks on a baking sheet coated with cooking spray. Bake at 375° for 13 minutes or until golden. Serve warm. **Serves 12 (serving size: 1 breadstick).**

CALORIES 84; FAT 2.2g (sat 1.1g, mono 0.5g, poly 0.3g); PROTEIN 3.3g; CARB 12.6g; FIBER 0.4g; CHOL 3mg; IRON 0.8mg; SODIUM 257mg; CALC 15mg

■ SHORTCUT TIP

Using high-quality ingredients (like intensely flavorful prosciutto) and fresh herbs (like rosemary) is an easy way to transform convenient premade dough into a delicious bread that's ready in minutes.

Cheese Toast Sticks

1 (13.8-ounce) can refrigerated pizza crust dough
Cooking spray
¼ cup canola mayonnaise

½ cup (2 ounces) reduced-fat shredded sharp cheddar cheese
1 teaspoon dried Italian seasoning
¼ teaspoon freshly ground black pepper

1. Preheat oven to 400°. Unroll pizza dough onto a large baking sheet coated with cooking spray.

2. Spread mayonnaise evenly over dough. Combine cheese, seasoning, and pepper; sprinkle over mayonnaise. Bake at 400° for 14 minutes or until crust is golden and cheese melts; cut crust crosswise into 14 (1-inch-wide) strips. Cut strips in half. **Serves 28 (serving size: 1 breadstick).**

CALORIES 55; FAT 2.5g (sat 0.4g, mono 1.1g, poly 0.6g); PROTEIN 1.6g; CARB 6.8g; FIBER 0.2g; CHOL 2mg; IRON 0.4mg; SODIUM 131mg; CALC 29mg

■ SHORTCUT TIP

Use a pizza cutter to easily cut the cheese toast into sticks. Be sure to coat the baking pan with cooking spray to prevent the dough from sticking.

ROLLS & FLATBREADS

Chapatis

4.75 ounces whole-wheat flour (about 1 cup)	¾ cup warm water (100° to 110°)
3.5 ounces bread flour (about ¾ cup)	2 tablespoons olive oil
1 teaspoon fine sea salt	Cooking spray

1. Weigh or lightly spoon flours into dry measuring cups; level with a knife. Combine flours and salt in a large bowl. Stir in ¾ cup warm water and oil to form a thick dough; mix well.

2. Turn dough out onto a lightly floured surface. Knead until smooth and elastic (about 10 minutes). Cover and let rise at room temperature 1 hour.

3. Divide dough into 8 equal portions. Working with 1 portion at a time (cover remaining dough to keep from drying), shape each portion into a ball. Let rest 5 minutes.

4. Roll each ball into a 6-inch circle on a lightly floured surface.

5. Heat a large cast-iron skillet over medium-high heat. Spray pan with cooking spray. Working with 1 portion at a time, cook 3 minutes on each side or until lightly browned with dark spots. **Serves 8 (serving size: 1 chapati).**

CALORIES 127; FAT 3.6g (sat 0.5g, mono 2.5g, poly 0.3g); PROTEIN 4g; CARB 20.3g; FIBER 2.3g; CHOL 0mg; IRON 1.3mg; SODIUM 288mg; CALC 0mg

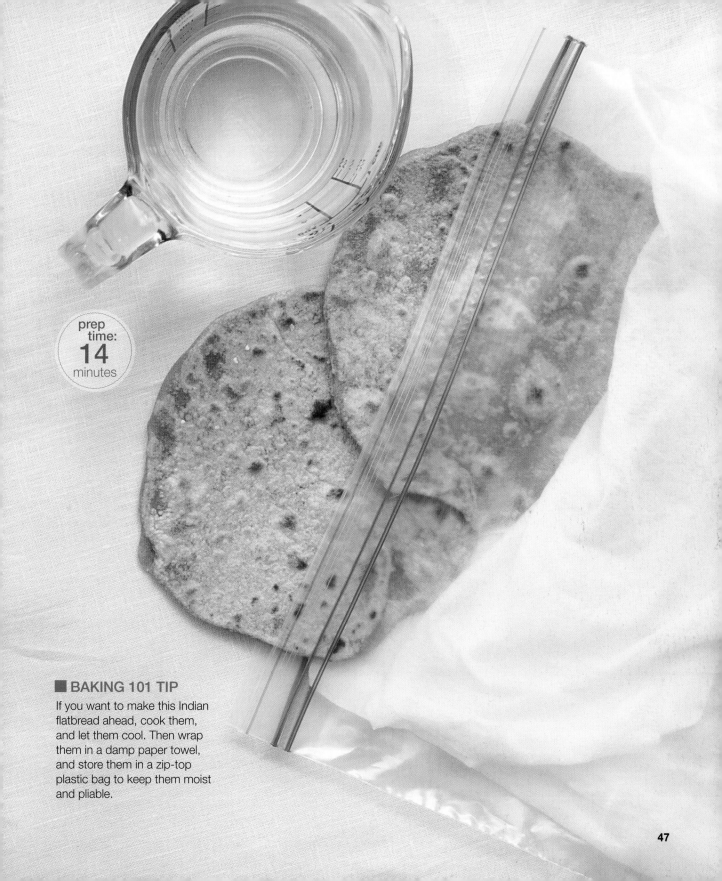

prep
time:
14
minutes

■ BAKING 101 TIP
If you want to make this Indian
flatbread ahead, cook them,
and let them cool. Then wrap
them in a damp paper towel,
and store them in a zip-top
plastic bag to keep them moist
and pliable.

Corn Tortillas

5.1 ounces masa harina (about 1½ cups)
1 cup plus 1 tablespoon water

½ teaspoon salt

1. Weigh or lightly spoon masa harina into dry measuring cups; level with a knife. Combine masa harina, 1 cup plus 1 tablespoon water, and salt in a large bowl, stirring with a whisk. Knead 30 seconds on a lightly floured surface. Cover and let stand 15 minutes.

2. Divide dough into 8 equal portions; shape each portion into a ball. Working with 1 dough ball at a time, place ball between 2 sheets of heavy-duty plastic wrap (cover remaining balls to prevent drying). Place ball, still covered, on a tortilla press. Close press to flatten dough, moving handle from side to side. Open press; turn dough one-half turn.

3. Close press to flatten. Remove dough. Carefully remove plastic wrap from flattened dough. Place between 2 sheets of wax paper. Repeat procedure with remaining dough balls.

4. Heat a large nonstick skillet over medium-high heat. Place 1 tortilla in pan; cook 1 minute or until it begins to brown. Carefully turn tortilla over; cook 1 minute. Turn tortilla once more, and cook 15 seconds. Repeat procedure with remaining tortillas. **Serves 8 (serving size: 1 tortilla).**

CALORIES 83; FAT 1g (sat 0.2g, mono 0.2g, poly 0.6g); PROTEIN 2.1g; CARB 17.8g; FIBER 1.9g; CHOL 0mg; IRON 0.7mg; SODIUM 148mg; CALC 43mg

■ SHORTCUT TIP

Use a tortilla press to quickly prep these tortillas. (They're available at kitchen stores and online for about $20.) In a pinch, use a rolling pin as a substitute. Masa harina is sold in many supermarkets; you'll find it by the flour or in the Latin food aisle.

prep time:
23
minutes

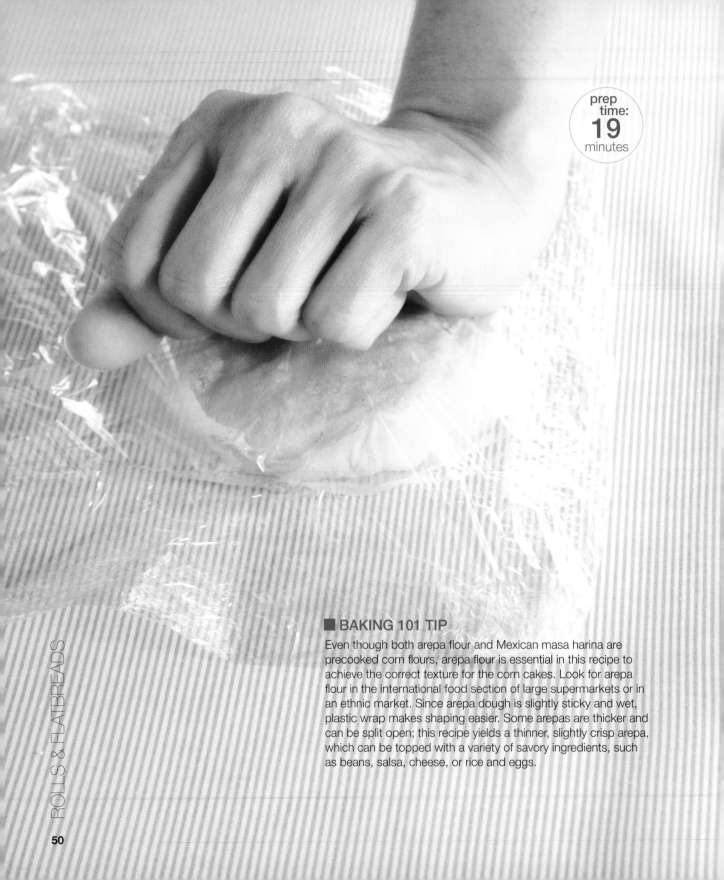

prep
time:
19
minutes

■ BAKING 101 TIP

Even though both arepa flour and Mexican masa harina are precooked corn flours, arepa flour is essential in this recipe to achieve the correct texture for the corn cakes. Look for arepa flour in the international food section of large supermarkets or in an ethnic market. Since arepa dough is slightly sticky and wet, plastic wrap makes shaping easier. Some arepas are thicker and can be split open; this recipe yields a thinner, slightly crisp arepa, which can be topped with a variety of savory ingredients, such as beans, salsa, cheese, or rice and eggs.

Arepas

5 **ounces yellow arepa flour (harina precocida; about 1 cup)**
½ **teaspoon salt**

1½ **cups boiling water**
Cooking spray

1. Weigh or lightly spoon flour into a dry measuring cup; level with a knife. Combine flour and salt in a large bowl. Add 1½ cups boiling water; stir with a wooden spoon until well combined and smooth (about 1 minute). Cover and let stand 5 minutes.

2. Scrape dough out onto a sheet of plastic wrap. Shape dough into a 2-inch-thick disk. Cut dough into 6 equal portions. Working with 1 dough portion at a time, place dough portion between 2 sheets of plastic wrap; shape into a ball, and flatten with palm of hand into a 3-inch circle (about ½ inch thick); shape edges to smooth.

3. Preheat oven to 350°. Heat a large skillet over medium heat. Coat arepas with cooking spray. Add arepas to pan, and cook 5 minutes on each side or until arepas begin to brown and a crust forms. Transfer arepas to a baking sheet coated with cooking spray. Bake at 350° for 15 minutes or until arepas sound hollow when lightly tapped.

Serves 6 (serving size: 1 arepa).

CALORIES 69; FAT 0.7g (sat 0.1g, mono 0.2g, poly 0.3g); PROTEIN 1.8g; CARB 14.5g; FIBER 1.8g; CHOL 0mg; IRON 1.4mg; SODIUM 200mg; CALC 29mg

Mexican Salsa Bread

1 (14-ounce) Italian cheese–flavored pizza crust
1 cup (4 ounces) shredded reduced-fat Monterey
   Jack cheese, divided

¾ cup picante sauce
⅓ cup chopped fresh cilantro

1. Preheat oven to 350°. Place pizza crust on a baking sheet.
2. Combine ½ cup cheese, picante sauce, and cilantro in a small bowl; stir well. Spread mixture over crust; sprinkle with remaining ½ cup cheese. Bake at 350° for 15 minutes or until cheese melts. Cut into 16 wedges. **Serves 16 (serving size: 1 wedge).**

CALORIES 89; FAT 2.8g (sat 1.3g, mono 0.4g, poly 0.1g); PROTEIN 4.4g; CARB 11.5g; FIBER 0.5g; CHOL 5mg; IRON 0.6mg; SODIUM 285mg; CALC 116mg

■ BAKING 101 TIP

The leaves of fresh cilantro are often mistaken for flat-leaf parsley, so read the tag to verify that you're buying the correct herb.

■ BAKING 101 TIP

Creating indentations in the surface of the dough prevents the dough from rising too much, giving this flatbread its characteristic appearance.

Caramelized Onion Flatbread

½ large sweet onion, thinly sliced
Olive oil–flavored cooking spray
½ cup water
2 garlic cloves, minced
1½ teaspoons dried Italian seasoning

¼ teaspoon freshly ground black pepper
1 (13.8-ounce) can refrigerated pizza crust dough
¼ cup (1 ounce) shredded Asiago or Parmesan cheese

1. Preheat oven to 450°. Lightly coat sliced onion with cooking spray. Heat a large skillet over medium-high heat. Add onion; sauté 5 minutes. Add 1 tablespoon water; cook until water evaporates. Repeat with remaining 7 tablespoons water, 1 tablespoon at a time, until onions are caramelized, scraping bottom of pan to loosen browned bits. Add garlic, Italian seasoning, and pepper; sauté 1 minute.

2. Unroll pizza crust dough. Place dough on a jelly-roll pan coated with cooking spray; press to within ½ inch of edges of pan. Press handle of a wooden spoon into dough to make indentations at 1-inch intervals. Spoon onion mixture and cheese over dough. Bake at 450° for 13 to 14 minutes or until crust is lightly browned. Cut into 10 equal pieces. **Serves 10 (serving size: 1 piece).**

CALORIES 113; FAT 2.3g (sat 0.8g, mono 0.7g, poly 0.4g); PROTEIN 3.7g; CARB 19.7g; FIBER 0.8g; CHOL 3mg; IRON 1.1mg; SODIUM 310mg; CALC 23mg

Roasted Garlic and Asiago Flatbread

1 (11-ounce) can refrigerated French bread dough

1 tablespoon extra-virgin olive oil, divided

1½ tablespoons bottled minced roasted garlic

¼ cup (1 ounce) shredded Asiago cheese

¼ cup (1 ounce) shredded part-skim mozzarella cheese

½ teaspoon freshly ground black pepper

1. Preheat oven to 375°. Unroll dough onto a baking sheet brushed with 1 teaspoon oil, and pat dough into a 16 x 12–inch rectangle.

2. Combine remaining 2 teaspoons oil and garlic, and brush over dough. Sprinkle with cheeses and pepper. Bake at 375° for 13 minutes or until golden brown. Remove from pan; cool slightly on a wire rack. Cut into 12 pieces.

Serves 12 (serving size: 1 piece).

CALORIES 92; FAT 3.3g (sat 1g, mono 1.1g, poly 0.2g); PROTEIN 3.1g; CARB 12.5g; FIBER 0.4g; CHOL 2mg; IRON 0.7mg; SODIUM 183mg; CALC 17mg

■ SHORTCUT TIP

Bottled minced roasted garlic is a true time-saver in the kitchen. Instead of having to roast a fresh clove and mince it, you can simply measure out the amount you need. However, if you have the time, you can always do this step yourself for fresher flavor.

Grissini

1 (11-ounce) can refrigerated French bread dough
2 tablespoons olive oil, divided
¼ cup (1 ounce) finely grated Parmigiano-Reggiano cheese

2 tablespoons lightly toasted sesame seeds
1 tablespoon poppy seeds
½ teaspoon freshly ground black pepper
¼ teaspoon kosher salt
Cooking spray

1. Preheat oven to 425°. Unroll dough into a rectangle on a lightly floured surface. Roll dough into a 15 x 13–inch rectangle. Brush dough evenly with 1 tablespoon oil. Combine cheese and next 4 ingredients, stirring well; sprinkle half of mixture evenly over dough, pressing gently to adhere. Turn dough over. Brush dough with remaining 1 tablespoon oil; sprinkle with remaining cheese mixture. Cut dough lengthwise into 48 thin strips (about ¼ inch thick) using a pizza cutter. Place strips in a single layer on baking sheets coated with cooking spray. Bake in batches at 425° for 4 minutes or until golden and crisp. **Serves 12 (serving size: 4 breadsticks).**

CALORIES 107; FAT 4.7g (sat 1.1g, mono 2.4g, poly 0.9g); PROTEIN 3.7g; CARB 12.8g; FIBER 0.3g; CHOL 2mg; IRON 0.9mg; SODIUM 249mg; CALC 52mg

■ BAKING 101 TIP

To vary the flavor, add crushed red pepper for some heat or finely chopped fresh herbs for color and flavor. You can also sub out the Parmigiano-Reggiano with other finely grated cheeses, such as Romano or Asiago.

Scones & Biscuits

Whole-Wheat Apple Scones

5 ounces all-purpose flour (about 1 cup plus 2 tablespoons)

4.75 ounces whole-wheat flour (about 1 cup)

¼ cup sugar

2 teaspoons baking powder

1 teaspoon ground cinnamon

½ teaspoon baking soda

½ teaspoon salt

Dash of ground nutmeg

¼ cup chilled butter, cut into small pieces

1 cup shredded peeled Granny Smith apple (about ½ pound)

½ cup 1% low-fat milk

1 teaspoon vanilla extract

Cooking spray

2 tablespoons 1% low-fat milk

2 teaspoons sugar

1. Preheat oven to 425°. Weigh or lightly spoon flours into dry measuring cups; level with a knife. Combine flours and next 6 ingredients in a large bowl; stir with a whisk. Cut in butter with a pastry blender or 2 knives until mixture resembles coarse meal. Add apple, ½ cup milk, and vanilla, stirring just until moist (dough will be sticky).
2. Turn dough out onto a lightly floured surface, and knead lightly 4 times with floured hands. Divide dough in half; pat each portion into a 6-inch circle on a baking sheet coated with cooking spray. Cut each circle into 5 wedges, cutting into but not through dough. Brush tops of wedges with 2 tablespoons milk, and sprinkle evenly with 2 teaspoons sugar. Bake at 425° for 15 minutes or until golden. **Serves 10 (serving size: 1 scone).**

CALORIES 170; FAT 5.1g (sat 3g, mono 1.3g, poly 0.3g); PROTEIN 3.7g; CARB 28.1g; FIBER 2.1g; CHOL 13mg; IRON 1.3mg; SODIUM 319mg; CALC 84mg

■ BAKING 101 TIP

Measuring flour is the single most important factor in light baking. Precision is crucial—too much and you'll have a dry product. Because of this, we prefer to measure flour by weight using a kitchen scale. If you don't have one, make sure you lightly spoon the flour into a dry measuring cup (don't scoop or pack it in the cup), and then level off the excess with a knife.

Glazed Apricot Scones

9 ounces all-purpose flour (about 2 cups)	½ cup 1% low-fat milk
2 tablespoons granulated sugar	1 large egg, lightly beaten
2½ teaspoons baking powder	2 tablespoons honey
¼ teaspoon salt	Cooking spray
3½ tablespoons chilled butter, cut into small pieces	½ cup powdered sugar
	2 teaspoons 1% low-fat milk
⅓ cup dried apricots, minced	1 tablespoon sliced almonds, toasted

1. Preheat oven to 375°. Weigh or lightly spoon flour into dry measuring cups; level with a knife. Combine flour and next 3 ingredients in a large bowl. Cut in butter with a pastry blender or 2 knives until mixture resembles coarse meal. Stir in apricots.

2. Combine ½ cup milk, egg, and honey in a small bowl. Add to flour mixture, stirring just until moist.

3. Turn dough out onto a lightly floured surface; knead lightly 4 to 5 times with floured hands. Pat dough into a 7-inch circle on a baking sheet coated with cooking spray. Cut dough into 10 wedges, cutting into but not through dough.

4. Bake at 375° for 20 minutes or until lightly browned. Remove to a wire rack over wax paper; cool 10 minutes. Combine powdered sugar and 2 teaspoons milk, stirring until smooth. Drizzle over warm scones, and sprinkle with almonds. **Serves 10 (serving size: 1 scone).**

CALORIES 202; FAT 5.3g (sat 2.9g, mono 1.5g, poly 0.4g); PROTEIN 4g; CARB 35g; FIBER 1.1g; CHOL 33mg; IRON 1.4mg; SODIUM 201mg; CALC 88mg

■ BAKING 101 TIP

Cutting in the butter using a pastry blender (or two knives, which just takes a little longer) evenly distributes the butter throughout the flour mixture and creates similarly sized pieces of butter. When these little pockets of butter melt while baking, the moisture contained in them produces steam, creating delicious flaky layers.

SCONES & BISCUITS

Banana Bran Scones

4.5 ounces all-purpose flour (about 1 cup)
½ cup oat bran
2 tablespoons chilled butter, cut into small pieces
1 teaspoon baking powder
¼ teaspoon baking soda
¼ teaspoon salt
¼ teaspoon ground cinnamon
¾ cup ripe mashed banana (about 2)
1 tablespoon brown sugar
¼ cup nonfat buttermilk
1½ teaspoons nonfat buttermilk
1½ teaspoons granulated sugar

1. Preheat oven to 400°. Weigh or lightly spoon flour into a dry measuring cup; level with a knife. Place flour and next 6 ingredients in a food processor; pulse until mixture resembles coarse meal.

2. Combine banana and brown sugar in a medium bowl; let stand 5 minutes. Add flour mixture and ¼ cup buttermilk alternately to banana mixture, stirring just until moist.

3. Turn dough out onto a lightly floured surface; knead lightly 4 to 5 times with floured hands. Pat dough into a 6-inch circle on a baking sheet lined with parchment paper. Cut dough into 8 wedges, cutting into but not through dough. Brush 1½ teaspoons buttermilk over surface of dough; sprinkle with granulated sugar. Bake at 400° for 12 minutes or until lightly browned. Remove from pan; cool on wire racks. **Serves 8 (serving size: 1 scone).**

CALORIES 126; FAT 3.5g (sat 1.9g, mono 0.9g, poly 0.4g); PROTEIN 3.2g; CARB 23.2g; FIBER 1.9g; CHOL 8mg; IRON 1.2mg; SODIUM 204mg; CALC 54mg

■ BAKING 101 TIP

Don't cut the dough into separate wedges before baking. By cutting into but not through the dough, the wedges bake as one large scone. They will be much moister than if they were baked separately. Lightly coat the knife with cooking spray to help prevent sticking.

Blueberry-Pecan Scones

½ cup 2% reduced-fat milk
¼ cup sugar
2 teaspoons grated lemon rind
1 teaspoon vanilla extract
1 large egg
9 ounces all-purpose flour (about 2 cups)
1 tablespoon baking powder
½ teaspoon salt
3 tablespoons chilled butter, cut into small pieces
1 cup fresh or frozen blueberries
¼ cup finely chopped pecans, toasted
Cooking spray
1 large egg white, lightly beaten
2 tablespoons sugar

1. Preheat oven to 375°. Combine first 5 ingredients in a medium bowl, stirring with a whisk. Weigh or lightly spoon flour into dry measuring cups; level with a knife. Combine flour, baking powder, and salt in a large bowl, stirring with a whisk. Cut in butter with a pastry blender or 2 knives until mixture resembles coarse meal. Gently fold in blueberries and pecans. Add milk mixture, stirring just until moist (dough will be sticky).
2. Turn dough out onto a floured surface. Pat dough into an 8-inch circle on a baking sheet coated with cooking spray. Cut dough into 10 wedges, cutting into but not through dough. Brush egg white over dough wedges; sprinkle evenly with 2 tablespoons sugar. Bake scones at 375° for 18 minutes or until golden. Serve warm. **Serves 10 (serving size: 1 scone).**

CALORIES 196; FAT 6.5g (sat 2.7g, mono 2.3g, poly 0.9g); PROTEIN 4.4g; CARB 30.3g; FIBER 1.4g; CHOL 31mg; IRON 1.4mg; SODIUM 281mg; CALC 97mg

■ BAKING 101 TIP

Scones, like biscuits, are most tender when handled minimally. So have your ingredients ready, and use a soft touch when mixing and patting the dough. For this recipe, resist the temptation to knead the dough; doing so would break apart the tender blueberries.

prep
time:
25
minutes

Toasted Almond and Cherry Scones

4.5 ounces all-purpose flour (about 1 cup)
3.3 ounces whole-wheat pastry flour (about ¾ cup)
½ cup old-fashioned rolled oats
¼ cup packed brown sugar
2 teaspoons baking powder
½ teaspoon baking soda
½ teaspoon salt
½ teaspoon ground cinnamon
¼ teaspoon ground allspice
5 tablespoons chilled butter, cut into small pieces
1 cup fat-free sour cream
1 teaspoon vanilla extract
⅓ cup chopped dried cherries
⅓ cup chopped natural almonds, toasted
Cooking spray
½ cup powdered sugar
1 tablespoon 2% reduced-fat milk

1. Preheat oven to 400°. Weigh or lightly spoon flours into dry measuring cups; level with a knife. Place oats in a food processor; process until finely ground. Add flours and next 6 ingredients to processor; pulse 3 times. Add butter; pulse 5 times or until mixture resembles coarse meal. Add sour cream and vanilla; pulse 3 times or just until combined (do not overmix). Add cherries and nuts; pulse 2 times.
2. Turn dough out onto a lightly floured surface; knead lightly 3 times. Roll dough to a ½-inch thickness; cut with a 2½-inch biscuit cutter to form 10 rounds. Place rounds 1 inch apart on a baking sheet lightly coated with cooking spray. Bake at 400° for 14 minutes or until golden brown. Remove from baking sheet; cool on a wire rack over wax paper.
3. Combine powdered sugar and milk, stirring with a whisk. Drizzle powdered sugar glaze over scones. **Serves 10 (serving size: 1 scone).**

CALORIES 258; FAT 8.7g (sat 3.9g, mono 3.1g, poly 0.9g); PROTEIN 5.7g; CARB 39.3g; FIBER 3.1g; CHOL 19mg; IRON 1.6mg; SODIUM 363mg; CALC 140mg

■ SHORTCUT TIP

Using a food processor in place of a pastry blender (or two knives) to blend the dough is a real time-saver. You can use it to quickly prepare the dough for any scone recipe.

Pistachio-Cranberry Scones

- 9 ounces all-purpose flour (about 2 cups)
- 2½ teaspoons baking powder
- ¼ teaspoon salt
- 5 tablespoons chilled butter, cut into small pieces
- ⅓ cup nonfat buttermilk
- ¼ cup granulated sugar
- 3 tablespoons honey
- 2 teaspoons grated lemon rind
- 1 large egg, lightly beaten
- ⅓ cup sweetened dried cranberries
- ¼ cup chopped pistachios, toasted
- 1 large egg white, lightly beaten
- 2 tablespoons turbinado sugar

1. Preheat oven to 400°. Weigh or lightly spoon flour into dry measuring cups; level with a knife. Combine flour, baking powder, and salt in a large bowl; cut in butter with a pastry blender or 2 knives until mixture resembles coarse meal. Cover and chill flour mixture 10 minutes.

2. Combine buttermilk and next 4 ingredients, stirring with a whisk until well blended. Stir in cranberries and nuts. Add buttermilk mixture to flour mixture; stir just until dough is moist.

3. Turn dough out onto a lightly floured surface. Pat dough into an 8-inch circle on a baking sheet lined with parchment paper. Cut dough into 12 wedges, cutting into but not through dough. Brush egg white over dough; sprinkle evenly with turbinado sugar. Bake at 400° for 13 minutes or until golden. Remove from pan; cool 2 minutes on wire racks. **Serves 12 (serving size: 1 scone).**

CALORIES 191; FAT 6.4g (sat 3.3g, mono 2g, poly 0.6g); PROTEIN 3.9g; CARB 29.9g; FIBER 1g; CHOL 30mg; IRON 1.3mg; SODIUM 184mg; CALC 66mg

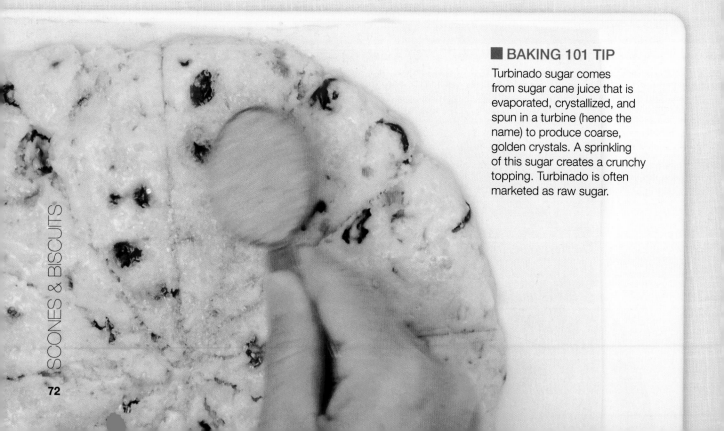

■ BAKING 101 TIP

Turbinado sugar comes from sugar cane juice that is evaporated, crystallized, and spun in a turbine (hence the name) to produce coarse, golden crystals. A sprinkling of this sugar creates a crunchy topping. Turbinado is often marketed as raw sugar.

prep
time:
15
minutes

73

SCONES & BISCUITS

Nectarine-Oatmeal Scones

5.6 ounces all-purpose flour (about 1¼ cups)
⅓ cup granulated sugar
2 teaspoons baking powder
½ teaspoon baking soda
¼ teaspoon salt
¼ cup chilled butter, cut into small pieces

1 cup old-fashioned rolled oats
½ cup low-fat buttermilk
1½ cups chopped nectarines (about 3 small)
Cooking spray
1 tablespoon turbinado sugar

1. Preheat oven to 425°. Weigh or lightly spoon flour into dry measuring cups; level with a knife. Combine flour and next 4 ingredients in a large bowl. Cut in butter with a pastry blender or 2 knives until mixture resembles coarse meal. Stir in oats. Add buttermilk to flour mixture, stirring just until moist. Gently fold in nectarines.

2. Turn dough out onto a lightly floured surface; knead lightly 3 or 4 times with floured hands. Pat dough into a 7-inch circle on a baking sheet coated with cooking spray. Cut dough into 10 wedges, cutting into but not through dough. Lightly coat tops of scones with cooking spray; sprinkle with turbinado sugar. Bake at 425° for 20 minutes or until lightly browned. **Serves 10 (serving size: 1 scone).**

CALORIES 182; FAT 5.7g (sat 3.1g, mono 1.5g, poly 0.5g); PROTEIN 3.6g; CARB 30.2g; FIBER 2g; CHOL 13mg; IRON 1.2mg; SODIUM 248mg; CALC 69mg

■ BAKING 101 TIP

We chose nectarines over peaches for this recipe because nectarines release less juice when baked than peaches. Extra juice will make the scones too wet and gummy.

Pear and Cardamom Scones

6.75	ounces all-purpose flour (about 1½ cups)	10	tablespoons low-fat buttermilk
2.4	ounces whole-wheat flour (about ½ cup)	1	teaspoon grated lemon rind
¼	cup sugar	1	teaspoon vanilla extract
2	teaspoons baking powder	1	large egg, lightly beaten
½	teaspoon salt	1	cup chopped fresh firm pear
⅛	teaspoon ground cardamom	2	teaspoons all-purpose flour
3	tablespoons chilled butter, cut into small pieces		Cooking spray
		1	large egg white, lightly beaten

1. Preheat oven to 350°. Weigh or lightly spoon flours into dry measuring cups; level with a knife. Combine flours and next 4 ingredients in a large bowl; cut in butter with a pastry blender or 2 knives until mixture resembles coarse meal.
2. Combine buttermilk and next 3 ingredients in a medium bowl; stir in pear. Add buttermilk mixture to flour mixture, stirring just until moist (dough will be sticky).
3. Turn dough out onto a lightly floured surface. Dust top of dough with 2 teaspoons all-purpose flour. Pat dough into an 8-inch circle on a baking sheet coated with cooking spray. Cut dough into 8 wedges, cutting into but not through dough. Brush egg white over dough. Bake at 350° for 25 minutes or until golden. **Serves 8 (serving size: 1 scone).**

CALORIES 228; FAT 5.7g (sat 3.1g, mono 1.6g, poly 0.4g); PROTEIN 5.7g; CARB 39.5g; FIBER 2.6g; CHOL 39mg; IRON 1.8mg; SODIUM 349mg; CALC 105mg

■ BAKING 101 TIP
Cardamom has a strong spicy-sweet flavor and a unique aroma. A little goes a long way.

■ SHORTCUT TIP

Using canned pumpkin instead of fresh helps cut down on the prep time of this recipe. The pumpkin mixture makes these scones moist and tender, and it imbues them with the antioxidant beta-carotene.

ORGANIC
Pumpkin

prep
time:
24
minutes

Pumpkin-Parmesan Scones

6.75 ounces all-purpose flour (about 1½ cups)
2.4 ounces whole-wheat flour (about ½ cup)
  2 teaspoons baking powder
  ½ teaspoon baking soda
  ½ teaspoon salt
  ¼ cup chilled butter, cut into small pieces

  ½ cup canned pumpkin
  ½ cup plain fat-free yogurt
  2 large egg whites, divided and lightly beaten
  2 tablespoons grated fresh Parmesan cheese
  1 tablespoon pumpkinseed kernels

1. Preheat oven to 400°. Weigh or lightly spoon flours into dry measuring cups; level with a knife. Combine flours and next 3 ingredients in a large bowl; cut in butter with a pastry blender or 2 knives until mixture resembles coarse meal. Combine pumpkin, yogurt, and 1 egg white, stirring with a whisk. Add to flour mixture; stir just until moist.

2. Turn dough out onto a lightly floured surface; knead lightly 4 times with floured hands. Pat dough into an 8-inch circle on a baking sheet lined with parchment paper. Cut dough into 12 wedges, cutting into but not through dough. Brush remaining 1 egg white over top of dough. Sprinkle dough with cheese and pumpkinseeds, pressing lightly to adhere. Bake at 400° for 20 minutes or until golden. **Serves 12 (serving size: 1 scone).**

CALORIES 129; FAT 4.9g (sat 2.7g, mono 1.2g, poly 0.5g); PROTEIN 4.4g; CARB 17.6g; FIBER 1.4g; CHOL 11mg; IRON 1.3mg; SODIUM 253mg; CALC 83mg

SCONES & BISCUITS

Yogurt–Green Onion Scones

6.75 ounces all-purpose flour (about 1½ cups)	½ teaspoon salt
2.4 ounces whole-wheat flour (about ½ cup)	¼ cup chilled butter, cut into small pieces
1 tablespoon sugar	½ cup thinly sliced green onions
2 teaspoons baking powder	¾ cup plain fat-free yogurt
½ teaspoon baking soda	1 large egg white

1. Preheat oven to 425°. Weigh or lightly spoon flours into dry measuring cups; level with a knife. Combine flours and next 4 ingredients in a large bowl; cut in butter with a pastry blender or 2 knives until mixture resembles coarse meal. Stir in onions. Combine yogurt and egg white, stirring with a whisk. Add to flour mixture, stirring just until moist (dough will be sticky).

2. Turn dough out onto a lightly floured surface; knead lightly 4 times with floured hands. Pat dough into an 8-inch circle on a baking sheet lined with parchment paper. Cut dough into 12 wedges, cutting into but not through dough. Bake at 425° for 15 minutes or until golden. **Serves 12 (serving size: 1 scone).**

CALORIES 121; FAT 4g (sat 2.4g, mono 1g, poly 0.3g); PROTEIN 3.3g; CARB 18.3g; FIBER 1.1g; CHOL 10mg; IRON 1.1mg; SODIUM 273mg; CALC 72mg

■ BAKING 101 TIP

Whole-wheat flour contains the vitamins and oil-rich germ of the wheat berry, which makes it nutritionally superior to refined white flour but also more sensitive to storage conditions. If you use whole-wheat flour often, store it in an airtight container in a cool, dry place. If you use it infrequently, store it in your freezer.

Cornmeal, Jalapeño, and Fresh Corn Scones

7.75 ounces all-purpose flour (about 1¾ cups)
¾ cup cornmeal
1 tablespoon baking powder
1 teaspoon kosher salt
4½ tablespoons chilled butter, cut into small pieces
½ cup fresh corn kernels (about 1 ear)
2 tablespoons finely chopped seeded jalapeño pepper
1 cup nonfat buttermilk
Cooking spray

1. Preheat oven to 400°. Weigh or lightly spoon flour into dry measuring cups; level with a knife. Combine flour and next 3 ingredients in a medium bowl, stirring with a whisk. Cut in butter with a pastry blender or 2 knives until mixture resembles coarse meal. Stir in corn and pepper. Add buttermilk, stirring just until moist (dough will be slightly sticky).

2. Turn dough out onto a lightly floured surface, and knead lightly 2 or 3 times with lightly floured hands. Pat dough into a 9-inch circle on a baking sheet coated with cooking spray. Cut dough into 12 wedges, cutting into but not through dough. Bake at 400° for 25 minutes or until lightly browned. Cool on a wire rack. **Serves 12 (serving size: 1 scone).**

CALORIES 150; FAT 4.8g (sat 2.8g, mono 1.2g, poly 0.3g); PROTEIN 3.6g; CARB 23.5g; FIBER 2.1g; CHOL 12mg; IRON 1.3mg; SODIUM 304mg; CALC 99mg

■ BAKING 101 TIP

Once baked, jalapeño peppers add relatively mild heat. If you want to tame the heat even further, reduce the amount of pepper or omit it. Substitute serrano chiles for a spicier version.

prep
time:
22
minutes

Manchego, Herb, and Sun-Dried Tomato Scones

9 ounces all-purpose flour (about 2 cups)
1½ teaspoons baking powder
¼ teaspoon salt
3 tablespoons chilled unsalted butter, cut into small pieces
½ cup chopped sun-dried tomatoes, packed without oil (2 ounces)

6 tablespoons shredded Manchego cheese
2 tablespoons chopped fresh basil
¾ cup nonfat buttermilk
2 large egg whites, lightly beaten
Cooking spray

1. Preheat oven to 425°. Weigh or lightly spoon flour into dry measuring cups; level with a knife. Combine flour, baking powder, and salt in a large bowl, stirring with a whisk. Cut in butter with a pastry blender or 2 knives until mixture resembles coarse meal. Stir in tomatoes, cheese, and basil. Add buttermilk and egg whites, stirring just until moist.

2. Turn dough out onto a lightly floured surface; knead lightly 4 times with floured hands. Pat dough into an 8-inch circle on a baking sheet coated with cooking spray. Cut dough into 8 wedges, cutting into but not through dough. Coat top of dough lightly with cooking spray. Bake at 425° for 15 minutes or until scones are golden. **Serves 8 (serving size: 1 scone).**

CALORIES 199; FAT 6.7g (sat 4.1g, mono 1.2g, poly 0.3g); PROTEIN 6.9g; CARB 27.6g; FIBER 1.3g; CHOL 17mg; IRON 1.8mg; SODIUM 289mg; CALC 152mg

■ BAKING 101 TIP

Since cheeses contain saturated fat, use those that have more flavor in small amounts. Spanish Manchego cheese adds mild, nutty notes and a salty punch to these scones. The longer the cheese has aged, the sharper the flavor. Ready-to-use sun-dried tomatoes don't require rehydration and add hearty flavor without extra fat.

Flaky Buttermilk Biscuits

9 ounces all-purpose flour (about 2 cups)
2½ teaspoons baking powder
½ teaspoon salt
5 tablespoons chilled butter, cut into small
  pieces

¾ cup nonfat buttermilk
3 tablespoons honey

1. Preheat oven to 400°. Weigh or lightly spoon flour into dry measuring cups; level with a knife. Combine flour, baking powder, and salt in a large bowl; cut in butter with a pastry blender or 2 knives until mixture resembles coarse meal. Chill 10 minutes.

2. Combine buttermilk and honey, stirring with a whisk until well blended. Add buttermilk mixture to flour mixture; stir just until moist.

3. Turn dough out onto a lightly floured surface; knead lightly 4 times. Roll dough into a (½-inch-thick) 9 x 5–inch rectangle; dust top of dough with flour. Fold dough crosswise into thirds (as if folding a piece of paper to fit into an envelope). Reroll dough into a (½-inch-thick) 9 x 5–inch rectangle; dust top of dough with flour. Fold dough cross-wise into thirds; gently roll or pat to a ¾-inch thickness. Cut dough with a 1¾-inch biscuit cutter to form 14 dough rounds. Place dough rounds, 1 inch apart, on a baking sheet lined with parchment paper. Bake at 400° for 12 minutes or until golden. Remove from pan; cool 2 minutes on wire racks. **Serves 14 (serving size: 1 biscuit).**

CALORIES 121; FAT 4.2g (sat 2.6g, mono 1.1g, poly 0.2g); PROTEIN 2.4g; CARB 18.4g; FIBER 0.5g; CHOL 11mg; IRON 0.9mg; SODIUM 198mg; CALC 63mg

■ BAKING 101 TIP

A light hand with the dough will help ensure tender biscuits. This method of folding the dough—folding it into thirds and rerolling—creates irresistible flaky layers.

honey

Seeded Cornmeal Biscuits

9 ounces all-purpose flour (about 2 cups)
9.5 ounces whole-wheat flour (about 2 cups)
1 cup stone-ground whole-grain cornmeal
¼ cup sugar
1 tablespoon baking soda
1 teaspoon baking powder
½ teaspoon salt

7 tablespoons chilled butter, cut into small pieces
2 cups low-fat buttermilk
Cooking spray
1 large egg white, lightly beaten
2 teaspoons poppy seeds
2 teaspoons sesame seeds

1. Preheat oven to 450°. Weigh or lightly spoon flours into dry measuring cups; level with a knife. Combine flours and next 5 ingredients in a large bowl; stir with a whisk. Cut in butter with a pastry blender or 2 knives until mixture resembles coarse meal. Add buttermilk; stir just until moist.

2. Turn dough out onto a lightly floured surface. Roll dough to a ¾-inch thickness; cut with a 2½-inch biscuit cutter into 18 biscuits. Gather remaining dough. Roll to a ¾-inch thickness, and cut with a 2½-inch biscuit cutter into 6 biscuits. Place 12 biscuits on a baking sheet coated with cooking spray. Brush tops of biscuits with half of egg white. Combine poppy seeds and sesame seeds in a small bowl, and sprinkle half of seed mixture evenly over biscuit tops. Bake at 450° for 10 minutes or until biscuits are golden; place on a wire rack. Repeat with remaining 12 biscuits, egg white, and seed mixture. **Serves 24 (serving size: 1 biscuit).**

CALORIES 139; FAT 4.2g (sat 2.3g, mono 1g, poly 0.3g); PROTEIN 3.7g; CARB 22.3g; FIBER 2.4g; CHOL 10mg; IRON 1.5mg; SODIUM 276mg; CALC 46mg

prep
time:
25
minutes

■ **BAKING 101 TIP**

Rerolling the dough is necessary to
maximize the number of biscuits you get,
but reroll only once. Overworked dough
yields tough biscuits. Bake one sheet of
biscuits at a time for the best results.

Purple Basil–Parmesan Biscuits

9   ounces all-purpose flour (about 2 cups)
2   tablespoons sugar
4   teaspoons baking powder
¼   teaspoon salt
¼   cup chilled unsalted butter, cut into small
     pieces

⅔   cup chopped fresh purple basil
½   cup (2 ounces) finely grated
     Parmigiano-Reggiano cheese
⅔   cup fat-free milk
1   large egg
     Cooking spray

1. Preheat oven to 425°. Weigh or lightly spoon flour into dry measuring cups; level with a knife. Combine flour and next 3 ingredients in a medium bowl, stirring with a whisk. Cut in butter with a pastry blender or 2 knives until mixture resembles coarse meal. Stir in basil and cheese. Combine milk and egg in a small bowl, stirring with a whisk. Add milk mixture to flour mixture; stir just until moist. Turn dough out onto a floured surface; pat to a 1-inch-thick circle. Cut with a 2-inch biscuit cutter into 12 biscuits. Place biscuits on a baking sheet coated with cooking spray. Bake at 425° for 15 minutes. Remove from oven, and cool. **Serves 12 (serving size: 1 biscuit).**

CALORIES 145; FAT 5.4g (sat 3.2g, mono 1.3g, poly 0.3g); PROTEIN 4.6g; CARB 19.5g; FIBER 0.7g; CHOL 31mg; IRON 1.3mg; SODIUM 276mg; CALC 156mg

prep
time:
20
minutes

■ **BAKING 101 TIP**

Fresh purple basil, which flecks these biscuits with color, offers mildly spicy hints of clove, licorice, mint, and cinnamon. Standard sweet Italian basil would do, as well.

Herb and Onion Wheat Biscuits

Cooking spray
 1 cup chopped onion
 ¾ cup fat-free milk
 6.75 ounces all-purpose flour (about 1½ cups)
 2.4 ounces whole-wheat flour (about ½ cup)
 2 teaspoons baking powder

 ½ teaspoon salt
 ¼ teaspoon sugar
 ¼ teaspoon dried oregano
 ¼ teaspoon dried basil
 ¼ cup chilled butter, cut into small pieces

1. Preheat oven to 425°. Heat a small skillet over medium heat. Coat pan with cooking spray. Add onion; cook 6 minutes or until tender, stirring frequently. Spoon onion into a blender. Add milk; process until smooth. Cool.
2. Weigh or lightly spoon flours into dry measuring cups; level with a knife. Combine flours and next 5 ingredients in a large bowl; cut in butter with a pastry blender or 2 knives until mixture resembles coarse meal. Add onion mixture; stir just until moist (dough will be sticky). Turn dough out onto a heavily floured surface, and knead lightly 5 times with floured hands. Roll dough to a ½-inch thickness; cut into 9 biscuits with a 3-inch biscuit cutter. Place on a baking sheet coated with cooking spray. Bake at 425° for 12 minutes or until golden. **Serves 9 (serving size: 1 biscuit).**

CALORIES 132; FAT 4.6g (sat 2.7g, mono 1.3g, poly 0.3g); PROTEIN 3.4g; CARB 19.9g; FIBER 1.4g; CHOL 12mg; IRON 1.2mg; SODIUM 252mg; CALC 81mg

■ BAKING 101 TIP

The onion is pureed so that its flavor
carries throughout the biscuits. You can
make and freeze the biscuits up to a week
ahead. When ready to serve, thaw, wrap
in foil, and heat in a 325° oven for 10 to
12 minutes or until thoroughly heated.

SCONES & BISCUITS

Spiced Pumpkin Biscuits

9 ounces all-purpose flour (about 2 cups)
2½ teaspoons baking powder
1¼ teaspoons pumpkin pie spice
½ teaspoon salt
5 tablespoons chilled butter, cut into small pieces

⅓ cup nonfat buttermilk
3 tablespoons honey
¾ cup canned pumpkin

1. Preheat oven to 400°. Weigh or lightly spoon flour into dry measuring cups; level with a knife. Combine flour and next 3 ingredients in a large bowl; cut in butter with a pastry blender or 2 knives until mixture resembles coarse meal. Chill 10 minutes.

2. Combine buttermilk and honey, stirring with a whisk until well blended; add canned pumpkin. Add buttermilk mixture to flour mixture; stir just until moist.

3. Turn dough out onto a lightly floured surface; knead lightly 4 times. Roll dough into a (½-inch-thick) 9 x 5–inch rectangle; dust top of dough with flour. Fold dough crosswise into thirds (as if folding a piece of paper to fit into an envelope). Reroll dough into a (½-inch-thick) 9 x 5–inch rectangle; dust top of dough with flour. Fold dough crosswise into thirds; gently roll or pat to a ¾-inch thickness. Cut dough with a 1¾-inch biscuit cutter to form 14 dough rounds. Place dough rounds, 1 inch apart, on a baking sheet lined with parchment paper. Bake at 400° for 14 minutes or until golden. Remove from pan; cool 2 minutes on wire racks. **Serves 14 (serving size: 1 biscuit).**

CALORIES 122; FAT 4.3g (sat 2.6g, mono 1.1g, poly 0.2g); PROTEIN 2.3g; CARB 18.9g; FIBER 0.9g; CHOL 11mg; IRON 1.1mg; SODIUM 192mg; CALC 59mg

■ BAKING 101 TIP

If your biscuits aren't rising properly, you might want to check the expiration date on your baking powder; it starts to weaken after 6 months. To check the strength, stir 2 teaspoons of baking powder into 1 cup of hot water. If there's an immediate fizz, the powder is fine.

Sweet Potato Biscuits

- **9 ounces all-purpose flour (about 2 cups)**
- **1 tablespoon sugar**
- **2 teaspoons baking powder**
- **½ teaspoon salt**
- **5 tablespoons chilled unsalted butter, cut into small pieces**
- **1 cup pureed cooked sweet potatoes, cooled**
- **⅓ cup fat-free milk**
- **Cooking spray**

1. Preheat oven to 400°. Weigh or lightly spoon flour into dry measuring cups; level with a knife. Combine flour and next 3 ingredients in a bowl. Cut in butter with a pastry blender or 2 knives until mixture resembles coarse meal. Combine sweet potato and milk in a small bowl; add potato mixture to flour mixture, stirring just until moist.

2. Turn dough out onto a lightly floured surface; knead lightly 5 times. Roll dough to a ¾-inch thickness; cut with a 2-inch biscuit cutter into 10 biscuits. Place biscuits on a baking sheet coated with cooking spray. Gather remaining dough. Roll to a ¾-inch thickness. Cut with a 2-inch biscuit cutter into 6 biscuits. Place biscuits on prepared baking sheet. Discard any remaining scraps.

3. Bake at 400° for 15 minutes or until lightly browned. Remove from pan; cool 5 minutes on wire racks. Serve warm or at room temperature. **Serves 16 (serving size: 1 biscuit).**

CALORIES 124; FAT 3.7g (sat 2.3g, mono 0.9g, poly 0.2g); PROTEIN 2.3g; CARB 20.1g; FIBER 1.3g; CHOL 9.5mg; IRON 1mg; SODIUM 173mg; CALC 47mg

prep
time:
20
minutes

■ **BAKING 101 TIP**

You'll need 1 medium sweet potato to yield 1 cup of
cooked pureed sweet potato for this recipe. Pierce
the sweet potato with a fork, and place it on a paper
towel. Microwave at HIGH 4 to 5 minutes or until
tender. Let the potato cool, and then mash using a
potato masher.

prep
time:
10
minutes

Cheddar-Bacon Drop Biscuits

9 ounces all-purpose flour (about 2 cups)
½ teaspoon baking soda
¼ teaspoon kosher salt
3½ tablespoons chilled butter, cut into small pieces
⅓ cup (1½ ounces) finely shredded sharp cheddar cheese

2 applewood-smoked bacon slices, cooked and crumbled
¾ cup nonfat buttermilk
¼ cup water
Cooking spray

1. Preheat oven to 400°. Weigh or lightly spoon flour into dry measuring cups; level with a knife. Combine flour, baking soda, and salt in a large bowl; stir with a whisk. Cut in butter with a pastry blender or 2 knives until mixture resembles coarse meal. Stir in cheese and bacon. Add buttermilk and ¼ cup water, stirring just until moist. Drop dough by 2 level tablespoonfuls 1 inch apart onto a baking sheet coated with cooking spray. Bake at 400° for 11 minutes or until golden brown. Serve warm. **Serves 18 (serving size: 1 biscuit).**

CALORIES 91; FAT 3.7g (sat 2.2g, mono 0.8g, poly 0.1g); PROTEIN 2.8g; CARB 11.5g; FIBER 0.4g; CHOL 10mg; IRON 0.7mg; SODIUM 127mg; CALC 32mg

■ BAKING 101 TIP

To make drop biscuits, you simply drop the dough onto the baking sheet. They have a higher proportion of liquid to dry ingredients than rolled biscuits, so you have a thick batter instead of a soft dough.

SCONES & BISCUITS

Asiago–Black Pepper Drop Biscuits

5.5 ounces all-purpose flour (about 1¼ cups)
1 teaspoon baking powder
½ teaspoon salt
¼ teaspoon cracked black pepper
1½ tablespoons chilled butter, cut into small pieces
½ cup (2 ounces) grated fresh Asiago cheese
¾ cup nonfat buttermilk
Cooking spray

1. Preheat oven to 450°. Weigh or lightly spoon flour into dry measuring cups; level with a knife. Combine flour and next 3 ingredients in a medium bowl; stir well with a whisk. Cut in butter with a pastry blender or 2 knives until mixture resembles coarse meal. Add cheese; toss well to combine. Add buttermilk; stir just until moist. Drop dough into 8 equal mounds on a baking sheet coated with cooking spray. Bake at 450° for 13 minutes or until edges are lightly browned. **Serves 8 (serving size: 1 biscuit).**

CALORIES 126; FAT 4.3g (sat 2.4g, mono 1.4g, poly 0.2g); PROTEIN 4.9g; CARB 16.7g; FIBER 0.6g; CHOL 12mg; IRON 1mg; SODIUM 285mg; CALC 134mg

■ BAKING 101 TIP

These savory biscuits are incredibly easy to make, as there's no need to roll or cut out the dough. If the batter seems too thick, you can add another tablespoon of nonfat buttermilk.

Muffins

Double-Apple Bran Muffins

Cooking spray
½ cup packed brown sugar
¼ cup butter, softened
1 large egg
1 large egg white
¾ cup fat-free milk
¼ cup applesauce
1 tablespoon molasses
½ teaspoon vanilla extract

4.5 ounces all-purpose flour (about 1 cup)
1½ cups oat bran
1½ teaspoons baking powder
¾ teaspoon salt
½ teaspoon ground cinnamon
½ cup coarsely chopped peeled Granny Smith apple
2 teaspoons turbinado sugar (optional)

1. Preheat oven to 400°. Place 12 paper muffin cup liners in muffin cups; coat liners with cooking spray. Set aside. Combine brown sugar and butter in a medium bowl; beat with a mixer at medium-high speed until well blended (about 5 minutes). Add egg; beat 1 minute or until well blended. Beat in egg white until well blended. Add milk, applesauce, molasses, and vanilla; beat at low speed until well blended.

2. Weigh or lightly spoon flour into a dry measuring cup; level with a knife. Combine flour and next 4 ingredients in a large bowl; make a well in center of mixture. Add milk mixture to flour mixture, stirring just until moist. Gently stir in apple.

3. Spoon batter into prepared muffin cups. Sprinkle evenly with turbinado sugar, if desired. Bake at 400° for 18 minutes or until muffins spring back when touched lightly in center. Cool 5 minutes in pan on a wire rack.

Serves 12 (serving size: 1 muffin).

CALORIES 174; FAT 5.6g (sat 2.8g, mono 1.6g, poly 0.8g); PROTEIN 5.2g; CARB 32.5g; FIBER 3g; CHOL 28mg; IRON 1.9mg; SODIUM 258mg; CALC 80mg

■ BAKING 101 TIP
Apples and applesauce make these healthful muffins sweet and moist.

MUFFINS

Whole-Wheat Apricot Muffins

4.5 ounces all-purpose flour (about 1 cup)
3 ounces whole-wheat flour (about ⅔ cup)
½ cup sugar
1¼ teaspoons grated orange rind
1 teaspoon baking soda
¼ teaspoon salt

1 cup low-fat buttermilk
¼ cup butter, melted
½ teaspoon vanilla extract
1 large egg
1 cup finely chopped dried apricots
Cooking spray

1. Preheat oven to 375°. Weigh or lightly spoon flours into dry measuring cups; level with a knife. Combine flours and next 4 ingredients in a large bowl, stirring with a whisk; make a well in center of mixture. Combine buttermilk and next 3 ingredients, stirring well with a whisk until well blended; add to flour mixture, stirring just until moist. Fold in apricots.

2. Spoon batter into 12 muffin cups coated with cooking spray. Bake at 375° for 15 minutes or until muffins spring back when touched lightly in center. Remove muffins from pan; cool slightly on a wire rack. **Serves 12 (serving size: 1 muffin).**

CALORIES 167; FAT 4.7g (sat 2.6g, mono 1.3g, poly 0.3g); PROTEIN 3.6g; CARB 29g; FIBER 1.9g; CHOL 29mg; IRON 1.1mg; SODIUM 221mg; CALC 37mg

■ **BAKING 101 TIP**

These muffins are best served warm, so reheat them before serving if you've made them a day or two ahead. Wrap the muffins in foil, and heat at 350° for 10 to 15 minutes.

prep time:
15
minutes

■ BAKING 101 TIP

Walnuts add fiber, vitamin E, and healthy unsaturated fats to these muffins. English walnuts, the most common variety in supermarkets, provide nearly 20 percent of the adequate daily intake of heart-healthy omega-3 fats per serving.

Banana-Nut Muffins with Oatmeal Streusel

Muffins:

Cooking spray
6.75 ounces all-purpose flour (about 1½ cups)
2.5 ounces whole-wheat flour (about ½ cup)
⅔ cup packed brown sugar
2 teaspoons baking powder
¼ teaspoon ground cinnamon
¼ teaspoon salt
1 cup mashed ripe banana (about 2)
¾ cup 1% low-fat milk
3 tablespoons canola oil
½ teaspoon vanilla extract
1 large egg
¼ cup chopped walnuts, toasted

Streusel:

6 tablespoons old-fashioned rolled oats
1.5 ounces all-purpose flour (about ⅓ cup)
2 tablespoons brown sugar
2 tablespoons butter, softened
¼ teaspoon ground cinnamon

1. Preheat oven to 375°. Place 12 paper muffin cup liners in muffin cups; coat liners with cooking spray. Set aside.
2. To prepare muffins, weigh or lightly spoon 6.75 ounces all-purpose flour (about 1½ cups) and whole-wheat flour into dry measuring cups; level with a knife. Combine flours and next 4 ingredients in a large bowl, stirring well with a whisk; make a well in center of mixture. Combine banana and next 4 ingredients in a bowl, stirring with a whisk until well blended. Add to flour mixture. Stir just until moist; fold in walnuts. Spoon batter into prepared muffin cups.
3. To prepare streusel, combine oats and next 4 ingredients in a small bowl. Blend with a pastry blender or 2 knives until mixture resembles coarse meal. Sprinkle streusel over batter. Bake at 375° for 22 minutes or until a wooden pick inserted in center comes out clean. Cool 5 minutes in pan on a wire rack. **Serves 12 (serving size: 1 muffin).**

CALORIES 232; FAT 7.4g (sat 1.5g, mono 3g, poly 2.4g); PROTEIN 4.6g; CARB 38.1g; FIBER 2.1g; CHOL 22mg; IRON 1.5mg; SODIUM 157mg; CALC 86mg

Whole-Grain Blackberry Spice Muffins

Cooking spray
9 ounces all-purpose flour (about 2 cups)
1 cup old-fashioned rolled oats
1 cup packed dark brown sugar
1½ teaspoons baking powder
½ teaspoon baking soda
½ teaspoon salt

½ teaspoon apple pie spice
1 cup fat-free milk
3 tablespoons butter, melted
1 teaspoon vanilla extract
1 large egg, lightly beaten
1½ cups frozen blackberries, coarsely chopped
¼ cup granulated sugar

1. Preheat oven to 400°. Place 17 paper muffin cup liners in muffin cups; coat liners with cooking spray. Set aside.
2. Weigh or lightly spoon flour into dry measuring cups; level with a knife. Combine flour and next 6 ingredients in a large bowl, stirring well with a whisk. Make a well in center of mixture. Combine milk and next 3 ingredients in a small bowl; add to flour mixture, stirring just until moist. Gently fold in blackberries.
3. Spoon batter into prepared muffin cups. Bake at 400° for 16 minutes. Sprinkle muffins evenly with granulated sugar; bake 3 minutes or until muffins spring back when touched lightly in center. Cool 5 minutes in pans on wire racks. **Serves 17 (serving size: 1 muffin).**

CALORIES 177; FAT 3g (sat 1.2g, mono 1.1g, poly 0.4g); PROTEIN 3.5g; CARB 34.3g; FIBER 1.8g; CHOL 18mg; IRON 1.4mg; SODIUM 181mg; CALC 68mg

■ BAKING 101 TIP
Coarsely chop the frozen blackberries, and then place them back in the freezer until you're ready to stir them into the batter.

MUFFINS

prep
time:
9
minutes

prep time: 7 minutes

Spiced Blueberry Muffins

9 ounces all-purpose flour (about 2 cups)
¾ cup sugar
1 tablespoon baking powder
½ teaspoon salt
½ teaspoon ground cinnamon
⅛ teaspoon ground nutmeg
⅛ teaspoon ground cloves
1½ cups fresh or frozen blueberries
1 tablespoon all-purpose flour

⅓ cup butter, softened
1 (8-ounce) block fat-free cream cheese, softened
½ cup 2% reduced-fat milk
1 teaspoon vanilla extract
2 large eggs
Cooking spray
1½ tablespoons sugar

1. Preheat oven to 425°. Weigh or lightly spoon 9 ounces (about 2 cups) flour into dry measuring cups; level with a knife. Combine 9 ounces flour (about 2 cups) and next 6 ingredients in a large bowl, stirring with a whisk. Make a well in center of mixture. Place blueberries in a small bowl. Sprinkle 1 tablespoon flour over blueberries; toss to coat.
2. Place butter and cream cheese in a medium bowl; beat with a mixer at high speed 1 minute or until blended. Add milk, vanilla, and eggs to butter mixture; beat to combine. Add butter mixture to flour mixture; stir just until moist. Gently fold in blueberry mixture.
3. Spoon batter into 14 muffin cups coated with cooking spray. Sprinkle 1½ tablespoons sugar evenly over batter. Bake at 425° for 15 minutes or until muffins spring back when touched lightly in center. Cool 5 minutes in pans on wire racks. Remove muffins from pans; cool on wire racks. **Serves 14 (serving size: 1 muffin).**

CALORIES 192; FAT 5.5g (sat 3.1g, mono 1.6g, poly 0.4g); PROTEIN 5.5g; CARB 29.9g; FIBER 1g; CHOL 46mg; IRON 1.1mg; SODIUM 289mg; CALC 124mg

■ BAKING 101 TIP

Eat these beautiful muffins while they're warm, and they'll melt in your mouth. Fresh berries are best, but you can also use frozen.

Cranberry-Orange Muffins

9 ounces all-purpose flour (about 2 cups)
1 cup sugar, divided
1½ teaspoons baking powder
1 teaspoon salt
½ teaspoon baking soda
2 teaspoons grated orange rind
¾ cup fresh orange juice
¼ cup canola oil
1 large egg, lightly beaten
2 cups coarsely chopped fresh cranberries (about 8 ounces)
⅓ cup chopped walnuts, toasted
Cooking spray

1. Preheat oven to 400°. Weigh or lightly spoon flour into dry measuring cups; level with a knife. Set aside 1 tablespoon sugar. Combine flour, remaining sugar, baking powder, salt, and baking soda in a large bowl, stirring well with a whisk; make a well in center of mixture.

2. Combine rind and next 3 ingredients in a small bowl, stirring well with a whisk. Add to flour mixture, stirring just until moist. Fold in cranberries and walnuts.

3. Spoon batter into 16 muffin cups coated with cooking spray. Sprinkle evenly with reserved 1 tablespoon sugar. Bake at 400° for 15 minutes or until muffins spring back when touched lightly in center. Run a knife or spatula around outer edge of each muffin cup. Remove muffins from pans; cool on wire racks. **Serves 16 (serving size: 1 muffin).**

CALORIES 169; FAT 5.6g (sat 0.5g, mono 2.5g, poly 2.4g); PROTEIN 2.5g; CARB 27.9g; FIBER 1.3g; CHOL 2.4mg; IRON 1mg; SODIUM 236mg; CALC 35mg

■ BAKING 101 TIP

Orange juice and rind in the batter serve as a sweet contrast to the tart cranberries. Fresh cranberries are at their peak from October through December and are usually packaged in 12-ounce plastic bags, each of which equals about 3 cups of whole berries. When their short season passes, you can use frozen cranberries in place of fresh.

MUFFINS

Oat-Topped Fig Muffins

6.75 ounces all-purpose flour (about 1½ cups)
5.1 ounces whole-wheat pastry flour (about 1 cup)
½ cup sugar
1 teaspoon baking powder
1 teaspoon baking soda
½ teaspoon salt
1½ cups low-fat buttermilk
1¼ cups chopped dried figs

2 tablespoons canola oil
1 teaspoon vanilla extract
1 large egg
Cooking spray
⅓ cup packed brown sugar
¼ cup quick-cooking oats
1 tablespoon butter, melted

1. Preheat oven to 400°. Weigh or lightly spoon flours into dry measuring cups; level with a knife. Combine flours and next 4 ingredients in a large bowl, stirring with a whisk. Make a well in center of mixture.
2. Place buttermilk and next 4 ingredients in a food processor; process until well blended. Add fig mixture to flour mixture, stirring just until combined. Spoon batter into 14 muffin cups coated with cooking spray.
3. Combine brown sugar, oats, and butter in a small bowl; toss with a fork until combined. Sprinkle oat mixture evenly over batter. Bake at 400° for 18 minutes or until a wooden pick inserted in center comes out clean. Cool 5 minutes in pan on a wire rack. Remove muffins from pan, and cool completely on wire rack. **Serves 14 (serving size: 1 muffin).**

CALORIES 201; FAT 4.2g (sat 1.2g, mono 1.7g, poly 0.9g); PROTEIN 4.6g; CARB 37.7g; FIBER 2.6g; CHOL 20mg; IRON 1.5mg; SODIUM 241mg; CALC 86mg

prep
time:
25
minutes

■ BAKING 101 TIP

To enjoy these muffins to the fullest, serve them
warm with raspberry preserves or orange marmalade.
You can bake them the day before, cool to room
temperature, and store in an airtight container. Just
reheat briefly in the microwave.

■ **BAKING 101 TIP**

Filling the muffin cups three-fourths full is key—
you want the cups to be filled enough to create
a nice muffin top, but not so much that the batter
overflows the cup while rising.

MUFFINS

Mini Lemon–Poppy Seed Muffins

Cooking spray
7.8 ounces all-purpose flour (about 1¾ cups)
¾ cup sugar
2½ teaspoons baking powder
½ teaspoon baking soda
½ teaspoon salt

1 tablespoon grated lemon rind
1 tablespoon poppy seeds
1¼ cups low-fat buttermilk
2 tablespoons butter, melted
1 large egg, lightly beaten

1. Preheat oven to 400°. Place 36 paper miniature muffin cup liners in miniature muffin cups; coat liners with cooking spray. Set aside.

2. Weigh or lightly spoon flour into dry measuring cups; level with a knife. Combine flour and next 4 ingredients in a medium bowl, stirring well with a whisk. Stir in lemon rind and poppy seeds; make a well in center of mixture. Combine buttermilk, butter, and egg, stirring well with a whisk. Add to flour mixture, stirring just until moist.

3. Spoon batter into prepared muffin cups, filling three-fourths full. Bake at 400° for 15 to 17 minutes or until golden brown. Cool 10 minutes in pans on wire racks. Remove muffins from pan; cool completely on wire racks. **Serves 36 (serving size: 1 mini muffin).**

CALORIES 51; FAT 1g (sat 0.5g, mono 0.2g, poly 0.1g); PROTEIN 1.2g; CARB 9.4g; FIBER 0.2g; CHOL 8mg; IRON 0.3mg; SODIUM 94mg; CALC 31mg

Pear and Walnut Muffins

Cooking spray
½ cup chopped walnuts, toasted
4.5 ounces all-purpose flour (about 1 cup)
1.5 ounces whole-wheat flour (about ⅓ cup)
1½ teaspoons baking powder
½ teaspoon baking soda
½ teaspoon salt

1 cup plain fat-free yogurt
⅔ cup packed brown sugar
2 tablespoons canola oil
2 teaspoons vanilla extract
1 large egg
1½ cups finely diced peeled pear
3 tablespoons turbinado sugar

1. Preheat oven to 400°. Place 15 paper muffin cup liners in muffin cups; coat liners with cooking spray. Set aside. Place walnuts in a food processor; process until finely ground.

2. Weigh or lightly spoon flours into dry measuring cups; level with a knife. Combine flours and next 3 ingredients in a medium bowl, stirring well with a whisk. Stir in ground walnuts. Make a well in center of mixture. Combine yogurt and next 4 ingredients in a small bowl; add to flour mixture, stirring just until moist. Fold in pear.

3. Spoon batter into prepared muffin cups; sprinkle batter with turbinado sugar. Bake at 400° for 20 minutes or until muffins spring back when touched lightly in center. Remove from pans immediately; cool on wire racks. Serve warm or at room temperature. **Serves 15 (serving size: 1 muffin).**

CALORIES 152; FAT 5.2g (sat 0.5g, mono 1.7g, poly 2.5g); PROTEIN 3.3g; CARB 24.2g; FIBER 1.3g; CHOL 14mg; IRON 0.8mg; SODIUM 190mg; CALC 77mg

■ BAKING 101 TIP

Fragrant pears and rich walnuts make an unbeatable combination. For this recipe, you can use any type of pear available; we suggest Anjou or Bartlett.

Tropical Muffins with Coconut-Macadamia Topping

Muffins:

- 6 ounces all-purpose flour (about 1⅓ cups)
- 1 cup old-fashioned rolled oats
- 1 teaspoon baking powder
- ½ teaspoon baking soda
- ½ teaspoon salt
- 1 cup mashed ripe banana (about 2)
- 1 cup low-fat buttermilk
- ½ cup packed brown sugar
- 2 tablespoons canola oil
- 1 teaspoon vanilla extract
- 1 large egg
- ½ cup canned crushed pineapple in juice, drained
- ⅓ cup flaked sweetened coconut
- 3 tablespoons finely chopped macadamia nuts, toasted
- Cooking spray

Topping:

- 2 tablespoons flaked sweetened coconut
- 1 tablespoon finely chopped macadamia nuts
- 1 tablespoon granulated sugar
- 1 tablespoon old-fashioned rolled oats

1. Preheat oven to 400°. To prepare muffins, weigh or lightly spoon flour into dry measuring cups; level with a knife. Combine flour and next 4 ingredients in a large bowl, stirring well with a whisk. Make a well in center of flour mixture. Combine banana and next 5 ingredients in a medium bowl, stirring with a whisk until well blended; add to flour mixture, stirring just until moist. Stir in pineapple, ⅓ cup coconut, and 3 tablespoons nuts. Spoon batter into 12 muffin cups coated with cooking spray.

2. To prepare topping, combine 2 tablespoons coconut and next 3 ingredients in a small bowl. Sprinkle about 1 teaspoon of topping over each muffin. Bake at 400° for 18 minutes or until muffins spring back when touched lightly in center. Remove muffins from pan immediately; cool on a wire rack. **Serves 12 (serving size: 1 muffin).**

CALORIES 205; FAT 6.7g (sat 1.7g, mono 3.4g, poly 1g); PROTEIN 4.3g; CARB 33.3g; FIBER 2g; CHOL 19mg; IRON 1.5mg; SODIUM 215mg; CALC 69mg

prep time: 20 minutes

■ BAKING 101 TIP

Flaked sweetened coconut is high in saturated fat for a plant food (nearly 94 percent of the fat is saturated), but a little offers tropical sweet flavor to the batter and texture to the topping. Most of the monounsaturated fat in each serving comes from mild-flavored canola oil and rich macadamia nuts.

prep
time:
15
minutes

Whole-Wheat, Oatmeal, and Raisin Muffins

Cooking spray
4.75 ounces whole-wheat flour (about 1 cup)
¼ cup granulated sugar
¼ cup packed brown sugar
2 tablespoons untoasted wheat germ
2 tablespoons wheat bran
1½ teaspoons baking soda
1 teaspoon ground cinnamon
½ teaspoon salt

1½ cups quick-cooking oats
⅓ cup chopped pitted dates
⅓ cup raisins
⅓ cup dried cranberries
1 cup low-fat buttermilk
¼ cup canola oil
1 teaspoon vanilla extract
1 large egg, lightly beaten
½ cup boiling water

1. Preheat oven to 375°. Place 12 paper muffin cup liners in muffin cups; coat liners with cooking spray. Set aside.
2. Weigh or lightly spoon flour into a dry measuring cup; level with a knife. Combine flour and next 7 ingredients in a large bowl, stirring with a whisk. Stir in oats and next 3 ingredients. Make a well in center of mixture. Combine buttermilk and next 3 ingredients; add to flour mixture, stirring just until moist. Stir in ½ cup boiling water. Let batter stand 15 minutes.
3. Spoon batter into prepared muffin cups. Bake at 375° for 20 minutes or until muffins spring back when touched lightly in center. Remove muffins from pan immediately; cool on a wire rack. **Serves 12 (serving size: 1 muffin).**

CALORIES 204; FAT 6.4g (sat 0.8g, mono 3.2g, poly 1.8g); PROTEIN 4.6g; CARB 34.7g; FIBER 3.4g; CHOL 19mg; IRON 1.4mg; SODIUM 288mg; CALC 43mg

■ BAKING 101 TIP

Adding boiling water to the batter and allowing it to stand for 15 minutes before baking gives the hearty oats, wheat germ, and bran time to soak up the liquid, producing a more tender muffin.

MUFFINS

Raspberry-Almond Muffins

½ cup granulated sugar
½ cup packed brown sugar
2½ tablespoons almond paste
3 tablespoons butter, softened
2 large eggs
½ cup nonfat buttermilk
1 teaspoon vanilla extract
1 teaspoon fresh lemon juice

9 ounces all-purpose flour (about 2 cups)
½ teaspoon baking powder
½ teaspoon baking soda
¼ teaspoon salt
1½ cups fresh raspberries
Cooking spray
2 tablespoons turbinado sugar or granulated sugar

1. Preheat oven to 375°. Place first 3 ingredients in a food processor, and process until well blended. Add butter, and pulse 4 to 5 times or just until combined. Add eggs, 1 at a time, pulsing 1 or 2 times after each addition. Add buttermilk, vanilla, and lemon juice; pulse until blended.

2. Weigh or lightly spoon flour into dry measuring cups; level with a knife. Combine flour and next 3 ingredients in a large bowl, stirring with a whisk. Make a well in center of mixture. Add buttermilk mixture; stir just until moist. Gently fold in raspberries. Let batter stand 5 minutes.

3. Spoon batter into 12 muffin cups coated with cooking spray. Sprinkle batter evenly with turbinado sugar. Bake at 375° for 22 minutes or until muffins spring back when touched lightly in center. Remove muffins from pan immediately; cool on a wire rack. **Serves 12 (serving size: 1 muffin).**

CALORIES 215; FAT 5.1g (sat 2.2g, mono 1.6g, poly 0.5g); PROTEIN 4.1g; CARB 38.9g; FIBER 1.7g; CHOL 43mg; IRON 1.4mg; SODIUM 167mg; CALC 49mg

■ BAKING 101 TIP

You can substitute frozen raspberries for fresh. Don't thaw the berries before stirring them in, as they'll soften and bleed into the batter.

Ginger-Carrot Muffins

Cooking spray
- 9 ounces all-purpose flour (about 2 cups)
- ½ cup sugar
- 2 teaspoons baking soda
- 1 teaspoon ground ginger
- ¼ teaspoon salt
- ½ cup fat-free sour cream
- ¼ cup canola oil
- ¼ cup 1% low-fat milk
- 1 teaspoon vanilla extract
- 2 large egg whites
- 1 large egg
- 3 cups grated carrot (about 6 medium)
- ½ cup dried currants
- ¼ cup chopped pecans, toasted

1. Preheat oven to 350°. Place 18 paper muffin cup liners in muffin cups; coat liners with cooking spray. Set aside.

2. Weigh or lightly spoon flour into dry measuring cups; level with a knife. Combine flour and next 4 ingredients in a large bowl, stirring with a whisk. Make a well in center of mixture. Combine sour cream and next 5 ingredients, stirring well with a whisk; add to flour mixture, stirring just until moist. Add carrot, currants, and pecans; stir just until combined.

3. Spoon batter into prepared muffin cups. Bake at 350° for 25 minutes or until muffins spring back when touched lightly in center. Remove muffins from pans immediately, and cool on wire racks. **Serves 18 (serving size: 1 muffin).**

CALORIES 143; FAT 4.8g (sat 0.5g, mono 2.6g, poly 1.4g); PROTEIN 3g; CARB 22.4g; FIBER 1.3g; CHOL 12mg; IRON 0.9mg; SODIUM 207mg; CALC 27mg

■ BAKING 101 TIP

Canola oil creates a moist, tender crumb; its mild taste doesn't interfere with the sweetness of carrots and currants or the ginger's bite.

MUFFINS

Pumpkin-Cranberry Muffins

Cooking spray
6.75 ounces all-purpose flour (about 1½ cups)
 1 teaspoon baking soda
 ¾ teaspoon ground ginger
 ½ teaspoon baking powder
 ½ teaspoon ground cinnamon
 ¼ teaspoon salt
 ⅛ teaspoon ground cloves

 1 cup granulated sugar
 1 cup canned pumpkin
 ½ cup low-fat buttermilk
 ¼ cup packed brown sugar
 2 tablespoons canola oil
 1 large egg
 ⅔ cup sweetened dried cranberries, chopped

1. Preheat oven to 375°. Place 15 paper muffin cup liners in muffin cups; coat liners with cooking spray. Set aside.
2. Weigh or lightly spoon flour into dry measuring cups; level with a knife. Combine flour and next 6 ingredients, stirring well with a whisk. Combine granulated sugar and next 5 ingredients in a large bowl; beat with a mixer at medium speed until well blended (about 3 minutes). Add flour mixture to sugar mixture; beat at low speed just until combined. Fold in cranberries.
3. Spoon batter into prepared muffin cups. Bake at 375° for 25 minutes or until muffins spring back when touched lightly in center. Remove muffins from pans immediately; cool on wire racks. **Serves 15 (serving size: 1 muffin).**

CALORIES 162; FAT 2.8g (sat 0.3g, mono 1.3g, poly 0.7g); PROTEIN 2.2g; CARB 33g; FIBER 1.2g; CHOL 15mg; IRON 1mg; SODIUM 156mg; CALC 30mg

■ BAKING 101 TIP

You can bake these muffins up to one month in advance. Place completely cooled muffins in a heavy-duty zip-top plastic bag, seal, and freeze. Let the muffins thaw at room temperature, and then microwave at MEDIUM-HIGH about 30 seconds to heat thoroughly.

Peanut Butter and Jelly Muffins

4.5 ounces all-purpose flour (about 1 cup)
3.5 ounces whole-wheat flour (about ¾ cup)
¼ cup granulated sugar
¼ cup packed dark brown sugar
1 tablespoon baking powder
½ teaspoon salt
1¼ cups fat-free milk
⅓ cup creamy peanut butter
2 tablespoons butter, melted
1 teaspoon vanilla extract
2 large egg whites
Cooking spray
¼ cup strawberry jam

1. Preheat oven to 400°. Weigh or lightly spoon flours into dry measuring cups; level with a knife. Combine flours and next 4 ingredients in a large bowl, stirring with a whisk. Make a well in center of mixture. Combine milk and next 4 ingredients; add to flour mixture, stirring just until moist.

2. Spoon batter into 12 muffin cups coated with cooking spray. Fill each cup half full with batter. Spoon 1 teaspoon jam into each cup. Spoon remaining batter on top to cover jam. Bake at 400° for 20 minutes or until muffins spring back when touched lightly in center. Cool 5 minutes in pan on a wire rack. Remove from pan, and cool on wire rack. **Serves 12 (serving size: 1 muffin).**

CALORIES 185; FAT 5.8g (sat 2g, mono 2.3g, poly 1.2g); PROTEIN 5.2g; CARB 29.4g; FIBER 1.6g; CHOL 6mg; IRON 1.2mg; SODIUM 288mg; CALC 113mg

■ BAKING 101 TIP

Don't use a natural-style peanut butter in this recipe; it won't have enough sugar or fat to help the muffins rise.

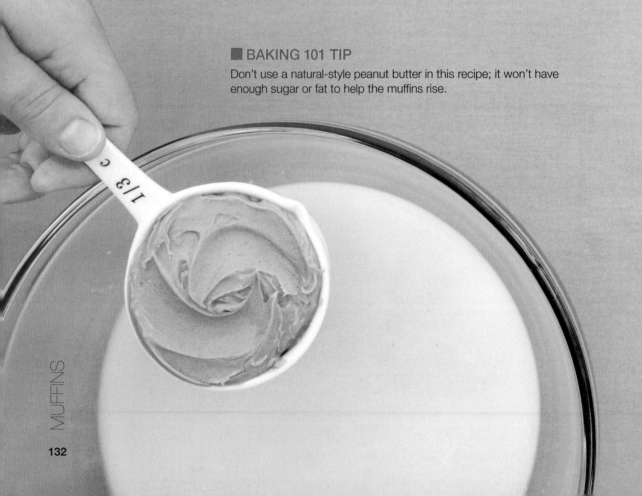

Honey and Toasted Pistachio Muffins

4.75 ounces whole-wheat flour (about 1 cup)
4.5 ounces all-purpose flour (about 1 cup)
¼ cup flaxseed meal
1¼ teaspoons baking soda
⅛ teaspoon salt
⅛ teaspoon ground nutmeg
⅛ teaspoon ground allspice
1 cup buttermilk

½ cup packed brown sugar
2 tablespoons canola oil
2 large eggs, lightly beaten
¼ cup golden raisins
Cooking spray
3 tablespoons finely chopped pistachios, toasted
2 tablespoons honey

1. Preheat oven to 350°. Weigh or lightly spoon flours into dry measuring cups; level with a knife. Combine flours and next 5 ingredients in a medium bowl, stirring well with a whisk. Make a well in center of mixture. Combine buttermilk, sugar, canola oil, and eggs; add to flour mixture, stirring just until moist. Stir in golden raisins.
2. Spoon batter into 12 muffin cups coated with cooking spray. Sprinkle evenly with pistachios. Bake at 350° for 15 minutes or until muffins spring back when touched lightly in center. Remove muffins from pan immediately; cool on a wire rack. Drizzle honey evenly over tops of muffins. Serve immediately. **Serves 12 (serving size: 1 muffin).**

CALORIES 198; FAT 6.2g (sat 1.1g, mono 2.4g, poly 2g); PROTEIN 5.2g; CARB 31.9g; FIBER 2.6g; CHOL 38mg; IRON 1.5mg; SODIUM 197mg; CALC 28mg

■ BAKING 101 TIP

Each of these healthy muffins contains almost 3 grams of fiber. Flaxseed meal provides a nutty flavor, fiber, and omega-3 fatty acids. Look for it in health-food stores and large supermarkets; it's also available online.

Ham and Cheese Corn Muffins

7.5 ounces all-purpose flour (about 1⅔ cups)
1 cup yellow cornmeal
1 tablespoon sugar
1¼ teaspoons baking soda
¼ teaspoon salt
⅛ teaspoon ground red pepper
1¼ cups low-fat buttermilk
3 tablespoons canola oil

4 large egg whites
¾ cup (3 ounces) reduced-fat shredded sharp cheddar cheese
½ cup finely chopped green onions
½ cup frozen whole-kernel corn, thawed
⅓ cup diced reduced-fat ham
Cooking spray

1. Preheat oven to 350°. Weigh or lightly spoon flour into dry measuring cups; level with a knife. Combine flour and next 5 ingredients in a medium bowl, stirring with a whisk. Make a well in center of mixture. Combine buttermilk, oil, and egg whites; add to flour mixture, stirring just until moist. Fold in cheese and next 3 ingredients.
2. Spoon batter into 12 muffin cups coated with cooking spray. Bake at 350° for 23 minutes or until a wooden pick inserted in center comes out clean. Remove muffins from pan; cool on a wire rack. **Serves 12 (serving size: 1 muffin).**

CALORIES 199; FAT 6.2g (sat 1.4g, mono 2.5g, poly 1.2g); PROTEIN 7.4g; CARB 28.2g; FIBER 1.3g; CHOL 9mg; IRON 1.7mg; SODIUM 290mg; CALC 141mg

■ SHORTCUT TIP
If you don't have buttermilk, make your own. Combine 1¼ cups of 1% low-fat milk and 4 teaspoons of lemon juice in a small bowl. Let the mixture stand for 5 minutes.

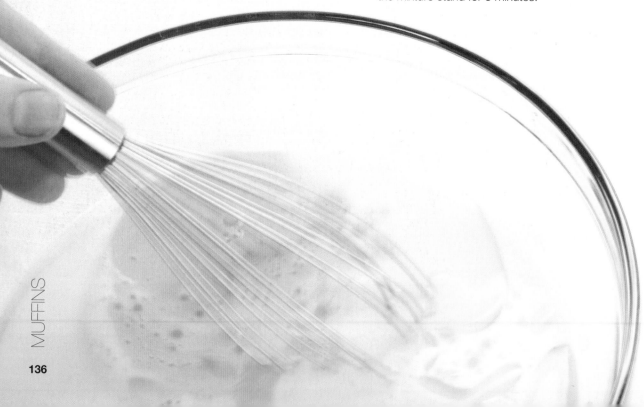

MUFFINS

prep
time:
15
minutes

Parmesan–Corn Bread Muffins

4.5 ounces all-purpose flour (about 1 cup)	⅔ cup nonfat buttermilk
⅔ cup yellow cornmeal	3 tablespoons canola oil
2 tablespoons sugar	2 large egg whites, lightly beaten
2 teaspoons baking powder	Cooking spray
¼ teaspoon salt	¼ cup (1 ounce) grated fresh Parmesan cheese

1. Preheat oven to 425°. Weigh or lightly spoon flour into dry measuring cups; level with a knife. Combine flour and next 4 ingredients in a medium bowl, stirring with a whisk. Make a well in center of mixture. Combine buttermilk, oil, and egg whites; add to flour mixture, stirring just until moist.

2. Spoon batter into 10 muffin cups coated with cooking spray. Sprinkle evenly with cheese. Bake at 425° for 10 minutes or until muffins spring back when touched lightly in center. Remove muffins from pan immediately; cool on a wire rack. Serve warm. **Serves 10 (serving size: 1 muffin).**

CALORIES 152; FAT 4.9g (sat 0.9g, mono 2.1g, poly 1.8g); PROTEIN 4.3g; CARB 21.9g; FIBER 0.6g; CHOL 2mg; IRON 1mg; SODIUM 229mg; CALC 110mg

■ BAKING 101 TIP

If using paper muffin cup liners, coat them with cooking spray before filling with batter to prevent bits of muffin from sticking. You can also use silicone liners. They work just like paper ones but are reusable.

■ BAKING 101 TIP

You can double this recipe and freeze the extra muffins for up to one month. Try Gruyère or Manchego in place of the cheddar cheese.

MUFFINS

Corn Bread Bites

3 ounces all-purpose flour (about ⅔ cup)
½ cup yellow cornmeal
1 tablespoon sugar
1½ teaspoons baking powder
¼ teaspoon salt
½ cup (2 ounces) shredded sharp cheddar
cheese

½ cup reduced-fat sour cream
¼ cup thinly sliced green onions
1 (8¾-ounce) can cream-style corn
Dash of hot sauce
1 large egg, lightly beaten
Cooking spray

1. Preheat oven to 375°. Weigh or lightly spoon flour into dry measuring cups; level with a knife. Combine flour and next 4 ingredients in a large bowl, stirring well with a whisk. Combine cheese and next 5 ingredients in a small bowl, stirring well with a whisk. Add to flour mixture; stir just until moist.

2. Spoon batter into 36 miniature muffin cups coated with cooking spray. Bake at 375° for 10 minutes or until golden brown. Cool 2 minutes in pans on wire racks. Remove muffins from pans; cool completely on wire racks. **Serves 12 (serving size: 3 muffins).**

CALORIES 108; FAT 3.4g (sat 1.9g, mono 0.5g, poly 0.1g); PROTEIN 3.7g; CARB 15.5g; FIBER 0.8g; CHOL 28mg; IRON 0.8mg; SODIUM 221mg; CALC 89mg

Millet Muffins with Honey-Pecan Butter

Muffins:

- ⅔ cup uncooked millet
- ¾ cup packed brown sugar
- 1 large egg
- 1 cup nonfat buttermilk
- 3 tablespoons butter, melted
- 6.75 ounces all-purpose flour (about 1½ cups)
- 1 teaspoon baking powder
- ¼ teaspoon baking soda
- ¼ teaspoon salt
- Cooking spray

Butter:

- 2 tablespoons butter, softened
- 2 tablespoons finely chopped pecans, toasted
- 1 tablespoon honey

1. Preheat oven to 375°. To prepare muffins, place millet in a spice or coffee grinder; pulse 6 times or until lightly crushed. Set aside.

2. Place sugar and egg in a large bowl; beat with a mixer at medium speed until well combined. Stir in millet, buttermilk, and 3 tablespoons butter.

3. Weigh or lightly spoon flour into dry measuring cups; level with a knife. Combine flour and next 3 ingredients, stirring with a whisk. Make a well in center of mixture. Add buttermilk mixture; stir just until moist. Let batter stand 5 minutes.

4. Spoon batter into 14 muffin cups coated with cooking spray. Bake at 375° for 18 minutes or until muffins spring back when touched lightly in center. Cool 5 minutes in pan on a wire rack. Remove muffins from pan; cool on wire rack.

5. To prepare butter, combine 2 tablespoons butter, pecans, and honey, stirring well to combine. Serve with muffins.

Serves 14 (serving size: 1 muffin and 1 teaspoon butter).

CALORIES 189; FAT 5.7g (sat 2.7g, mono 1.8g, poly 0.7g); PROTEIN 3.7g; CARB 31.1g; FIBER 1.3g; CHOL 26mg; IRON 1.3mg; SODIUM 237mg; CALC 57mg

■ BAKING 101 TIP

Look for millet, a round, pale yellow grain, in health-food stores or the organic sections of large supermarkets. If you don't have a spice grinder, pulse the millet in a mini food processor or blender, or lightly crush it with a mortar and pestle.

Quick
Bread Loaves &
Coffee Cakes

Banana Bread

3.6 ounces whole-wheat flour (about ¾ cup)
3.4 ounces all-purpose flour (about ¾ cup)
¼ cup flaxseed meal
1 teaspoon baking powder
½ teaspoon salt
½ teaspoon baking soda

1 cup mashed ripe banana (about 2 large)
¾ cup sugar
⅓ cup chopped walnuts
½ cup plain low-fat yogurt
¼ cup canola oil
Cooking spray

1. Preheat oven to 325°. Weigh or lightly spoon flours into dry measuring cups; level with a knife. Combine flours and next 4 ingredients in a large bowl, stirring with a whisk. Combine banana and next 4 ingredients in a small bowl. Add banana mixture to flour mixture, stirring just until moist.

2. Spoon batter into a 9 x 5–inch loaf pan coated with cooking spray. Bake at 325° for 1 hour or until a wooden pick inserted in center comes out clean. Cool 10 minutes in pan on a wire rack; remove from pan. Cool on wire rack.

Serves 12 (serving size: 1 slice).

CALORIES 201; FAT 8.2g (sat 0.7g, mono 3.5g, poly 3.4g); PROTEIN 4.1g; CARB 30.2g; FIBER 2.5g; CHOL 1mg; IRON 1mg; SODIUM 189mg; CALC 58mg

■ BAKING 101 TIP

Adding the wet ingredients to a well in the center of the dry ingredients allows you to stir smoothly, with no more mixing than necessary to blend the batter.

QUICK BREAD LOAVES & COFFEE CAKES

prep
time:
10
minutes

Fig, Date, and Walnut Quick Bread

¾ cup low-fat buttermilk

½ teaspoon finely grated lemon rind

¼ teaspoon ground nutmeg

⅛ teaspoon ground cloves

⅔ cup chopped dried figs

⅓ cup chopped pitted dates

½ cup packed brown sugar

2 tablespoons canola oil

2 large eggs

3.6 ounces whole-wheat flour (about ¾ cup)

3.4 ounces all-purpose flour (about ¾ cup)

1½ teaspoons baking soda

⅛ teaspoon salt

Cooking spray

⅓ cup chopped walnuts

1. Preheat oven to 350°. Heat first 4 ingredients in a small, heavy saucepan over medium heat just until bubbles begin to form around edge (do not boil). Remove from heat; stir in figs and dates. Let stand 20 minutes or until fruit softens.

2. Combine sugar, oil, and eggs in a large bowl; stir with a whisk until well blended. Stir in cooled buttermilk mixture.

3. Weigh or lightly spoon flours into dry measuring cups; level with a knife. Combine flours, baking soda, and salt in a large bowl; make a well in center of mixture. Add milk mixture to flour mixture, stirring just until moist. Spoon batter into an 8 x 4–inch loaf pan coated with cooking spray. Sprinkle walnuts evenly over batter. Bake at 350° for 40 minutes or until a wooden pick inserted in center comes out clean. Cool 10 minutes in pan on a wire rack; remove from pan. Cool completely on wire rack. **Serves 12 (serving size: 1 slice).**

CALORIES 192; FAT 5.8g (sat 0.8g, mono 2g, poly 2.5g); PROTEIN 4.4g; CARB 32.5g; FIBER 2.9g; CHOL 36mg; IRON 1.4mg; SODIUM 216mg; CALC 55mg

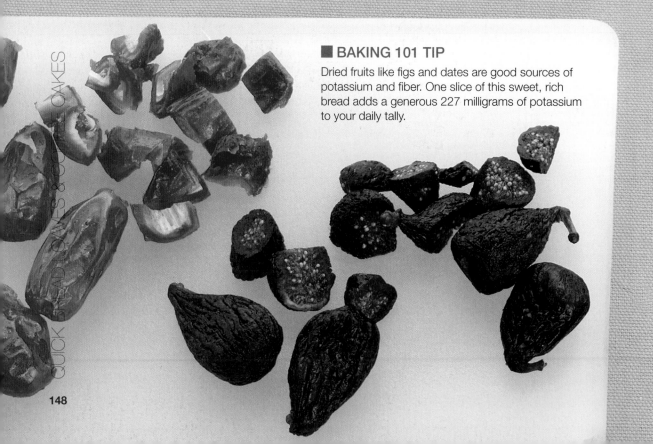

■ BAKING 101 TIP

Dried fruits like figs and dates are good sources of potassium and fiber. One slice of this sweet, rich bread adds a generous 227 milligrams of potassium to your daily tally.

QUICK BREADS, LOAVES & COFFEE CAKES

QUICK BREAD LOAVES & COFFEE CAKES

Orange-Coconut Bread

1 cup sugar	5 tablespoons flaked sweetened coconut, divided
1 tablespoon canola oil	2½ teaspoons grated orange rind
1 large egg	1 teaspoon baking soda
¼ cup 2% reduced-fat milk	½ teaspoon salt
1 (6-ounce) carton plain fat-free yogurt	Cooking spray
9 ounces all-purpose flour (about 2 cups)	

1. Preheat oven to 350°. Combine first 3 ingredients in a medium bowl, stirring with a whisk until smooth. Stir in milk and yogurt. Weigh or lightly spoon flour into dry measuring cups; level with a knife. Combine flour, ¼ cup coconut, orange rind, baking soda, and salt in a large bowl; make a well in center of mixture. Add milk mixture to flour mixture stirring just until moist.

2. Spoon batter into a 9 x 5–inch loaf pan coated with cooking spray. Sprinkle with remaining 1 tablespoon coconut. Bake at 350° for 50 minutes or until a wooden pick inserted in center comes out clean. Cool in pan 10 minutes.

Serves 12 (serving size: 1 slice).

CALORIES 178; FAT 2.6g (sat 1g, mono 1g, poly 0.5g); PROTEIN 4.1g; CARB 34.8g; FIBER 0.8g; CHOL 18mg; IRON 1.1mg; SODIUM 228mg; CALC 53mg

■ **BAKING 101 TIP**

When testing for doneness in a quick bread, there should be even browning and some resistance to light finger pressure. If your bread feels squishy, it isn't done. To check, pierce the bread in the center with a wooden pick, a bamboo skewer, or a long, skinny knife; it should come out clean with no batter attached.

Pecan-Topped Pumpkin Bread

15 **ounces all-purpose flour (about 3⅓ cups)**
 1 **tablespoon baking powder**
 2 **teaspoons baking soda**
 1 **teaspoon salt**
 1 **teaspoon ground cinnamon**
 1 **teaspoon ground nutmeg**
 ½ **teaspoon ground allspice**
 2 **cups sugar**
 ½ **cup canola oil**
 ½ **cup low-fat buttermilk**
 4 **large egg whites**
 2 **large eggs**
 ⅔ **cup water**
 1 **(15-ounce) can pumpkin**
   Cooking spray
 ⅓ **cup chopped pecans**

1. Preheat oven to 350°. Weigh or lightly spoon flour into dry measuring cups; level with a knife. Combine flour and next 6 ingredients in a bowl.

2. Place sugar and next 4 ingredients in a large bowl; beat with a mixer at high speed until well blended. Add ⅔ cup water and pumpkin, beating at low speed until blended. Add flour mixture to pumpkin mixture, beating at low speed just until moist.

3. Spoon batter into 2 (9 x 5–inch) loaf pans coated with cooking spray. Sprinkle pecans evenly over batter. Bake at 350° for 1 hour or until a wooden pick inserted in center comes out clean. Cool 10 minutes in pans on a wire rack; remove from pans. Cool completely on wire rack. **Serves 24 (serving size: 1 slice).**

CALORIES 198; FAT 6.6g (sat 0.7g, mono 3.6g, poly 1.9g); PROTEIN 3.4g; CARB 32.3g; FIBER 1.2g; CHOL 18mg; IRON 1.4mg; SODIUM 287mg; CALC 53mg

■ BAKING 101 TIP

Check the bread after 50 minutes of baking—you may need to cover the loaves with foil for the last 10 minutes to prevent overbrowning.

prep time: 10 minutes

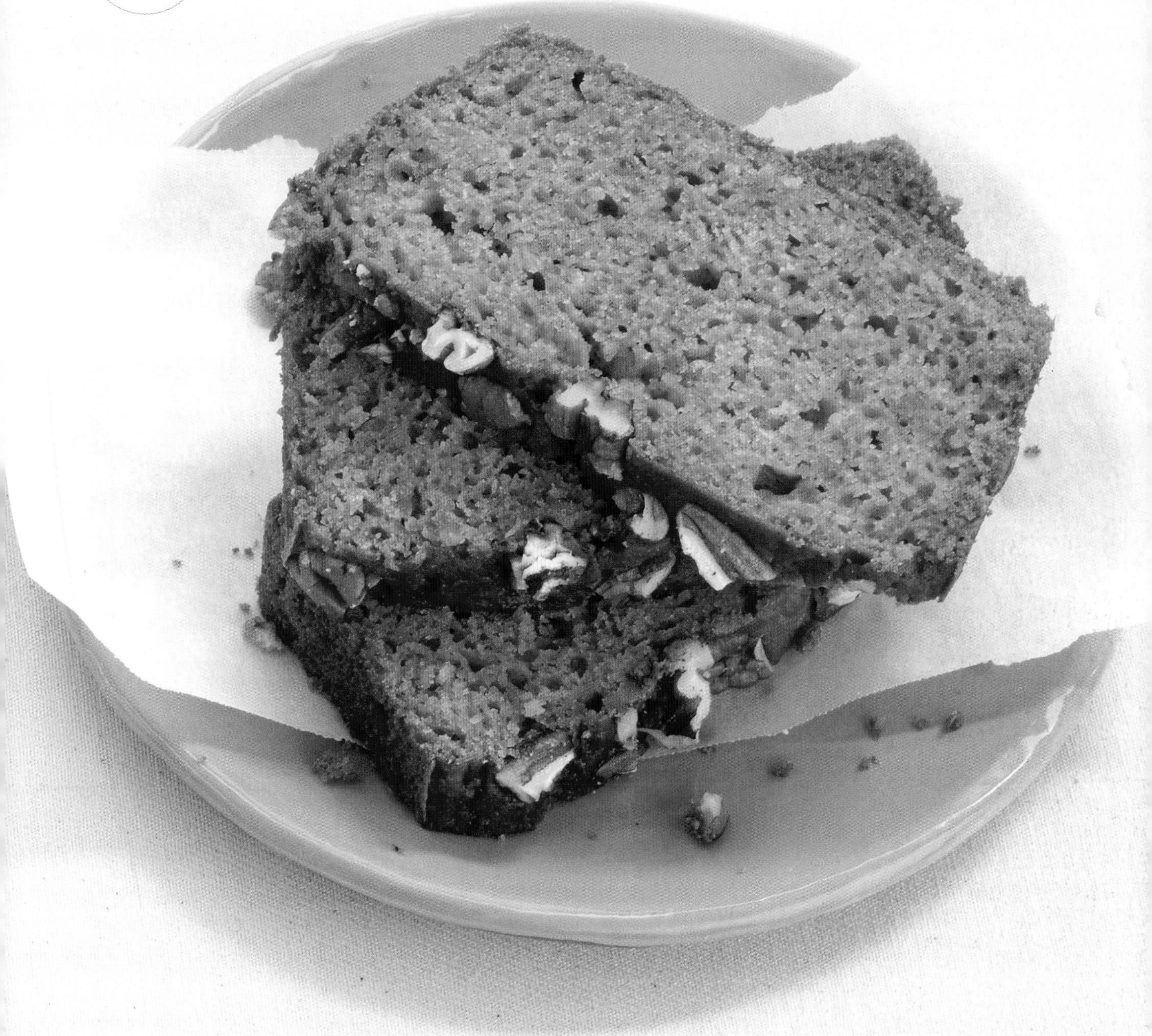

Zucchini-Pineapple Quick Bread

13.5 ounces sifted all-purpose flour (about 3 cups)
1½ teaspoons ground cinnamon
 1 teaspoon salt
 1 teaspoon baking soda
 ½ teaspoon baking powder
 2 large eggs
 2 cups sugar
 2 cups grated zucchini (about 1½ medium zucchini)

⅔ cup canola oil
 2 teaspoons vanilla extract
 4 large egg whites
 2 (8-ounce) cans crushed pineapple in juice, drained
Baking spray with flour

1. Preheat oven to 325°. Weigh or lightly spoon flour into dry measuring cups; level with a knife. Combine flour and next 4 ingredients in a large bowl, stirring well with a whisk.
2. Beat eggs with a mixer at medium speed until foamy. Add sugar and next 4 ingredients, beating until well blended. Add zucchini mixture to flour mixture, stirring just until moist. Fold in pineapple.
3. Spoon batter into 2 (9 x 5–inch) loaf pans coated with baking spray. Bake at 325° for 1 hour or until a wooden pick inserted in center comes out clean. Cool 10 minutes in pans on a wire rack; remove from pans. Cool completely on wire rack. **Serves 28 (serving size: 1 slice).**

CALORIES 167; FAT 5.9g (sat 0.5g, mono 3.3g, poly 1.7g); PROTEIN 2.4g; CARB 26.5g; FIBER 0.7g; CHOL 15mg; IRON 0.9mg; SODIUM 151mg; CALC 16mg

■ SHORTCUT TIP

Using canned pineapple instead of fresh cuts down on the prep time of this recipe. Make sure you buy a variety canned in its own juice. Those that are canned in light and heavy syrups contain added sugar and calories.

prep
time:
16
minutes

prep
time:
14
minutes

Mini Fruit and Sunflower Loaves

- 9 ounces all-purpose flour (about 2 cups)
- 1 cup yellow cornmeal
- 2 teaspoons baking soda
- ¼ teaspoon salt
- 2 cups vanilla fat-free yogurt
- ½ cup canola oil
- ½ cup maple syrup
- ½ cup honey
- 1 teaspoon vanilla extract
- 1 cup chopped dried mixed fruit
- ½ cup sunflower seed kernels
- 1 teaspoon grated orange rind
- Cooking spray

1. Preheat oven to 350°. Weigh or lightly spoon flour into dry measuring cups; level with a knife. Combine flour and next 3 ingredients in a large bowl; make a well in center of mixture. Combine yogurt and next 4 ingredients. Add yogurt mixture to flour mixture, stirring just until moist. Fold in fruit, sunflower seeds, and rind.

2. Spoon batter into 4 (6 x 2½–inch) loaf pans coated with cooking spray. Bake at 350° for 35 minutes or until a wooden pick inserted in center comes out clean. Remove from pans; cool completely on a wire rack. **Serves 24 (serving size: 1 slice).**

CALORIES 188; FAT 6.2g (sat 0.5g, mono 3.2g, poly 2.2g); PROTEIN 3.1g; CARB 30.8g; FIBER 1.1g; CHOL 0mg; IRON 1.1mg; SODIUM 145mg; CALC 37mg

■ BAKING 101 TIP

Sunflower seeds provide healthy unsaturated fats, the antioxidant vitamin E, iron, fiber, and folate, which is essential for pregnant women to help prevent birth defects.

Lemon, Thyme, and Cornmeal Quick Bread

1.5 ounces all-purpose flour (about ⅓ cup)
1 cup fine yellow cornmeal
1 teaspoon baking powder
¾ teaspoon kosher salt
⅔ cup sugar
⅓ cup plus 2 tablespoons canola oil
6 large egg whites

1 tablespoon chopped fresh thyme
1 tablespoon grated lemon rind
2 tablespoons fresh lemon juice
2 tablespoons pine nuts, toasted and divided
Cooking spray
1 tablespoon butter, melted

1. Preheat oven to 325°. Weigh or lightly spoon flour into a dry measuring cup; level with a knife. Combine flour and next 3 ingredients in a medium bowl, stirring with a whisk.

2. Place sugar, oil, and egg whites in a large bowl; beat with a mixer at medium-high speed 1 minute or until well blended. Add thyme, rind, and juice; beat at low speed until combined. Add flour mixture; beat just until combined. Chop 1 tablespoon nuts; stir into batter.

3. Pour batter into a 9 x 5–inch loaf pan coated with cooking spray. Sprinkle evenly with remaining 1 tablespoon whole nuts. Bake at 325° for 30 minutes. Remove pan from oven (do not turn oven off). Drizzle butter evenly over loaf. Bake an additional 20 minutes or until a wooden pick inserted in center comes out clean. Cool in pan 5 minutes on a wire rack; remove from pan. Cool completely on wire rack. **Serves 12 (serving size: 1 slice).**

CALORIES 207; FAT 10.5g (sat 1.3g, mono 5.6g, poly 3.1g); PROTEIN 3g; CARB 2.3g; FIBER 0.6g; CHOL 3mg; IRON 0.9mg; SODIUM 188mg; CALC 36mg

■ BAKING 101 TIP

Cornmeal is made from dried corn kernels that have been ground into a meal. It's ground into one of three textures—fine, medium, or coarse. For the best texture in this bread, be sure to choose regular or finely ground cornmeal. Avoid stone-ground cornmeal, as it is too coarse for this delicate bread.

prep time: **13** minutes

Steamed Brown Bread

4.75 ounces whole-wheat flour (about 1 cup)
4 ounces rye flour (about 1 cup)
1 cup cornmeal
1 cup raisins
2 teaspoons baking soda
½ teaspoon salt

2 cups buttermilk
¾ cup molasses
2 tablespoons butter, melted
1 tablespoon grated orange rind
Cooking spray

1. Preheat oven to 350°. Weigh or lightly spoon flours into dry measuring cups; level with a knife. Combine flours and next 4 ingredients in a large bowl, stirring with a whisk. Combine buttermilk and next 3 ingredients. Add buttermilk mixture to flour mixture; stir just until moist. Divide batter evenly between 2 (8 x 4–inch) loaf pans coated with cooking spray. Tightly cover each pan with foil. Place pans in a 13 x 9–inch metal baking pan. Add boiling water to a depth of 1 inch. Cover larger pan with foil.

2. Bake at 350° for 1 hour and 10 minutes or until a knife inserted in center comes out clean. (Top of bread will feel slightly sticky.) Remove pans from water; uncover. Cool 10 minutes on a wire rack. Remove from pans; cool completely on wire rack. **Serves 24 (serving size: 1 slice).**

CALORIES 124; FAT 1.9g (sat 1.1g, mono 0.3g, poly 1.2g); PROTEIN 2.5g; CARB 25.4g; FIBER 1.9g; CHOL 5mg; IRON 1.1mg; SODIUM 190mg; CALC 28mg

■ BAKING 101 TIP
Steaming the bread creates moist, dense loaves.

Brown Soda Bread

Cooking spray
11.25 ounces whole-wheat flour (about 2½ cups)
2.25 ounces all-purpose flour (about ½ cup)
½ cup steel-cut oats
2 tablespoons brown sugar
1 tablespoon wheat germ

1 teaspoon baking soda
1 teaspoon baking powder
½ teaspoon salt
2 cups low-fat buttermilk
1 large egg, lightly beaten

1. Preheat oven to 325°. Coat a 9 x 5–inch loaf pan with cooking spray. Line pan with parchment paper, and coat with cooking spray.

2. Weigh or lightly spoon flours into dry measuring cups; level with a knife. Combine flours and next 6 ingredients. Combine buttermilk and egg. Add buttermilk mixture to flour mixture; stir just until combined.

3. Spoon mixture into prepared pan. Bake at 325° for 1 hour and 5 minutes or until a wooden pick inserted in center comes out clean. Invert bread onto a wire rack; cool completely. **Serves 12 (serving size: 1 slice).**

CALORIES 160; FAT 1.8g (sat 0.5g, mono 0.2g, poly 0.3g); PROTEIN 7.2g; CARB 30.8g; FIBER 4g; CHOL 18mg; IRON 1.7mg; SODIUM 286mg; CALC 86mg

■ **BAKING 101 TIP**

Whole-wheat flour, wheat germ, and steel-cut oats (also called Irish oatmeal) make this version a healthy interpretation of the classic Irish bread.

Basic Beer-Cheese Bread

1 tablespoon olive oil
½ cup finely chopped yellow onion
¼ teaspoon freshly ground black pepper
1 garlic clove, minced
13.5 ounces all-purpose flour (about 3 cups)
3 tablespoons sugar
2 teaspoons baking powder

1 teaspoon salt
1 cup (4 ounces) shredded Monterey Jack cheese
1 (12-ounce) bottle lager-style beer
Cooking spray
2 tablespoons melted butter, divided

1. Preheat oven to 375°. Heat a small skillet over medium-low heat. Add oil to pan; swirl to coat. Add onion to pan; cook 10 minutes or until browned, stirring occasionally. Stir in pepper and garlic; cook 1 minute.

2. Weigh or lightly spoon flour into dry measuring cups; level with a knife. Combine flour and next 3 ingredients in a large bowl, stirring with a whisk; make a well in center of mixture. Add onion mixture, cheese, and beer to flour mixture, stirring just until moist.

3. Spoon batter into a 9 x 5–inch loaf pan coated with cooking spray. Drizzle 1 tablespoon butter over batter. Bake at 375° for 35 minutes. Drizzle remaining 1 tablespoon butter over loaf. Bake an additional 25 minutes or until top is golden brown and a wooden pick inserted in center comes out clean. Cool in pan 5 minutes on a wire rack; remove from pan. Cool completely on wire rack. **Serves 16 (serving size: 1 slice).**

CALORIES 144; FAT 4.4g (sat 2.4g, mono 1.6g, poly 0.2g); PROTEIN 4.3g; CARB 20.6g; FIBER 0.7g; CHOL 10mg; IRON 1.3mg; SODIUM 257mg; CALC 89mg

■ BAKING 101 TIP

Drizzling butter over the top of this quick bread twice gives it a wonderfully brown, crisp crust and a rich flavor, accentuating the cheese spread throughout the loaf. The bread is endlessly variable; you can change the type of beer or the cheese to make numerous combinations.

Kalamata Olive Bread with Oregano

1 tablespoon olive oil
1 cup finely chopped onion
9 ounces all-purpose flour (about 2 cups)
1 teaspoon baking soda
¼ teaspoon salt
1 cup low-fat buttermilk

2 tablespoons butter, melted
2 large egg whites
¼ cup pitted kalamata olives, chopped
1 tablespoon chopped fresh oregano
Cooking spray

1. Preheat oven to 350°. Heat a large nonstick skillet over medium-high heat. Add oil to pan; swirl to coat. Add onion to pan; sauté 3 minutes or until onion is tender. Set aside.

2. Weigh or lightly spoon flour into dry measuring cups; level with a knife. Combine flour, baking soda, and salt in a large bowl; make a well in center of mixture. Combine buttermilk, butter, and egg whites, stirring with a whisk. Add buttermilk mixture to flour mixture, stirring just until moist. Fold in onion, olives, and oregano.

3. Spread batter into an 8 x 4–inch loaf pan coated with cooking spray. Bake at 350° for 45 minutes or until a wooden pick inserted in center comes out clean. Cool 10 minutes in pan on a wire rack; remove from pan. Cool completely on wire rack. **Serves 12 (serving size: 1 slice).**

CALORIES 133; FAT 4.6g (sat 1.8g, mono 2.2g, poly 0.4g); PROTEIN 3.8g; CARB 18.8g; FIBER 0.8g; CHOL 6.7mg; IRON 1mg; SODIUM 255mg; CALC 39mg

■ **BAKING 101 TIP**

Kalamata olives provide rich flavor in this fragrant
loaf. You can substitute other varieties of olives for
the kalamata, if you like.

Chile-Cheese Corn Bread

⅓ cup unsalted butter, softened
2 tablespoons sugar
4 large egg whites
2 large eggs
⅓ cup nonfat buttermilk
3.3 ounces all-purpose flour (about ¾ cup)
1¾ cups cornmeal
1¼ teaspoons baking soda

1¼ teaspoons baking powder
¼ teaspoon salt
¾ cup (3 ounces) reduced-fat shredded extra-sharp cheddar cheese
1 (14.75-ounce) can cream-style corn
1 (4.5-ounce) can chopped green chiles, undrained
Cooking spray

1. Preheat oven to 375°. Combine softened butter and sugar in a large bowl; beat with a mixer at medium speed until light and fluffy. Add egg whites, eggs, and buttermilk, beating at low speed until well combined.
2. Weigh or lightly spoon flour into dry measuring cups; level with a knife. Combine flour and next 4 ingredients in a medium bowl, stirring with a whisk. Add flour mixture to buttermilk mixture, stirring just until combined. Fold in cheese, corn, and chiles.
3. Pour batter into a 10-inch cast-iron skillet coated with cooking spray. Bake at 375° for 45 minutes or until a wooden pick inserted in center comes out clean. Remove from oven, and cool 5 minutes in pan. **Serves 16 (serving size: 1 piece).**

CALORIES 180; FAT 6.1g (sat 3.5g, mono 1.2g, poly 0.3g); PROTEIN 5.3g; CARB 25.8g; FIBER 0.8g; CHOL 40mg; IRON 1.1mg; SODIUM 317mg; CALC 73mg

QUICK BREAD LOAVES & COFFEE CAKES

■ BAKING 101 TIP

If you don't have a cast-iron skillet, you can bake the bread at 375° in a 13 x 9–inch nonstick or dark metal baking pan coated with cooking spray for 45 minutes.

Banana Coffee Cake with Macadamia Nuts and Coconut

Cooking spray
6 ounces all-purpose flour (about 1⅓ cups)
½ teaspoon salt
½ teaspoon baking powder
¼ teaspoon baking soda
1 cup mashed ripe banana (about 2 large)
¾ cup granulated sugar
3 tablespoons canola oil
1 teaspoon vanilla extract

¼ teaspoon ground nutmeg
1 large egg
¼ cup packed dark brown sugar
1 tablespoon water
2 teaspoons butter
2 tablespoons chopped macadamia nuts, toasted
2 tablespoons flaked sweetened coconut

1. Preheat oven to 350°. Coat a 9-inch round cake pan with cooking spray; line bottom of pan with wax paper. Coat wax paper with cooking spray.

2. Weigh or lightly spoon flour into dry measuring cups; level with a knife. Combine flour and next 3 ingredients in a bowl, stirring with a whisk. Combine banana and next 5 ingredients in a large bowl; beat with a mixer at medium speed 1 minute or until well blended. Add flour mixture to banana mixture, and beat just until moist.

3. Pour batter into prepared pan. Bake at 350° for 30 minutes or until a wooden pick inserted in center comes out clean. Cool in pan 10 minutes on a wire rack; remove from pan. Carefully peel off wax paper.

4. Combine brown sugar, 1 tablespoon water, and butter in a small saucepan; bring to a boil. Cook 1 minute, stirring constantly. Remove from heat; stir in nuts and coconut. Spread over cake. **Serves 12 (serving size: 1 wedge).**

CALORIES 190; FAT 5.8g (sat 1.3g, mono 2.6g, poly 1.6g); PROTEIN 2.3g; CARB 32.6g; FIBER 1g; CHOL 19mg; IRON 0.9mg; SODIUM 159mg; CALC 22mg

■ BAKING 101 TIP

A banana is ripe when its yellow peel has a few brown spots. This is when it's also at its height of sweetness and provides the strongest banana flavor.

171

Blueberry-Lemon Coffee Cake

Cake:
- **6.75 ounces all-purpose flour (about 1½ cups)**
- **2 teaspoons baking powder**
- **½ teaspoon salt**
- **¼ teaspoon baking soda**
- **½ cup sugar**
- **⅓ cup almond paste**
- **2 tablespoons chilled butter, cut into small pieces**
- **1 tablespoon lemon juice**
- **1 large egg**
- **¾ cup fat-free milk**
- **1½ cups blueberries**
- **2 teaspoons grated lemon rind**
- **Cooking spray**

Topping:
- **¼ cup sugar**
- **3 tablespoons sliced almonds, chopped**
- **1½ tablespoons butter, melted**
- **½ teaspoon ground cinnamon**

1. Preheat oven to 350°. To prepare cake, weigh or lightly spoon flour into dry measuring cups; level with a knife. Combine flour and next 3 ingredients in a small bowl, stirring with a whisk.

2. Place ½ cup sugar, almond paste, and 2 tablespoons butter in a large bowl; beat with a mixer at medium speed until well blended. Add lemon juice and egg, beating well. Add flour mixture and milk alternately to sugar mixture, beginning and ending with flour mixture. Fold in blueberries and rind. Spoon batter into an 8-inch square metal baking pan coated with cooking spray.

3. To prepare topping, combine ¼ cup sugar and remaining ingredients in a small bowl, tossing with a fork until moist. Sprinkle topping evenly over batter. Bake at 350° for 35 minutes or until a wooden pick inserted in center comes out clean. Cool in pan on a wire rack. **Serves 12 (serving size: 1 piece).**

CALORIES 196; FAT 6.5g (sat 2.1g, mono 3.2g, poly 0.8g); PROTEIN 3.8g; CARB 31.6g; FIBER 1.4g; CHOL 27mg; IRON 1.2mg; SODIUM 243mg; CALC 82mg

■ **BAKING 101 TIP**

Almond paste, a sweet mixture of ground almonds and sugar, contributes a mildly nutty flavor and moist texture. You can find almond paste in the baking section of the grocery store. (Don't substitute marzipan, which is sweeter and has a smoother texture.) If the almond paste is hard, soften it by microwaving at HIGH 10 to 15 seconds.

prep
time:
20
minutes

Cherry Ripple Sour Cream Coffee Cake

Streusel:
- **2.25 ounces whole-wheat flour (about ½ cup)**
- **½ cup old-fashioned rolled oats**
- **½ cup packed brown sugar**
- **3 tablespoons chopped pecans**
- **1 teaspoon ground cinnamon**
- **2 tablespoons frozen orange juice concentrate, thawed**
- **1 tablespoon canola oil**

Cake:
- **Cooking spray**
- **¼ cup canola oil**
- **2 tablespoons butter, melted**
- **1 cup granulated sugar**
- **2 teaspoons vanilla extract**
- **1 large egg**
- **1 large egg white**
- **9 ounces all-purpose flour (about 2 cups)**
- **1 teaspoon baking soda**
- **1 teaspoon baking powder**
- **½ teaspoon salt**
- **1 cup fat-free sour cream**
- **2 cups pitted fresh cherries (about 10 ounces), coarsely chopped**

1. Preheat oven to 350°. To prepare streusel, weigh or lightly spoon whole-wheat flour into a dry measuring cup; level with a knife. Combine whole-wheat flour and next 4 ingredients. Add concentrate and 1 tablespoon oil; stir until crumbly.

2. To prepare cake, coat an 8-inch tube pan with cooking spray. Combine ¼ cup oil and melted butter in a medium bowl. Add granulated sugar, vanilla, egg, and egg white; beat with a mixer at medium speed until smooth.

3. Weigh or lightly spoon all-purpose flour into dry measuring cups; level with a knife. Combine all-purpose flour and next 3 ingredients in a large bowl. Add flour mixture and sour cream alternately to egg mixture, beginning and ending with flour mixture. Fold in cherries.

4. Spoon half of batter into prepared pan; sprinkle with half of streusel. Spoon in remaining batter; top with remaining streusel. Bake at 350° for 1 hour and 5 minutes or until a wooden pick inserted in center comes out clean. Cool in pan 10 minutes on a wire rack; run a knife around outside edge. Cool completely in pan. **Serves 16 (serving size: 1 piece).**

CALORIES 246; FAT 7.6g (sat 1.5g, mono 3.8g, poly 1.9g); PROTEIN 4g; CARB 41.5g; FIBER 1.8g; CHOL 18mg; IRON 1.4mg; SODIUM 227mg; CALC 53mg

■ **BAKING 101 TIP**

Cherry juice can stain fabrics and countertops, so be sure to chop the cherries near your sink.

Cranberry Upside-Down Coffee Cake

Cake:

Cooking spray

1 tablespoon all-purpose flour

1 cup fresh cranberries

½ cup coarsely chopped pitted dates

2 tablespoons chopped walnuts

1 teaspoon grated orange rind

½ cup butter, softened and divided

½ cup packed dark brown sugar

2 tablespoons fresh orange juice

¼ teaspoon ground cinnamon

6.75 ounces all-purpose flour (about 1½ cups)

1 teaspoon baking powder

½ teaspoon salt

1 cup granulated sugar

1 teaspoon vanilla extract

1 large egg

½ cup nonfat buttermilk

Glaze:

1 cup powdered sugar

2 tablespoons fresh orange juice

1 teaspoon butter, melted

1. Preheat oven to 350°. To prepare cake, coat an 8-inch square metal baking pan with cooking spray; dust with 1 tablespoon flour. Combine cranberries and next 3 ingredients in a bowl. Melt 2 tablespoons butter in a small saucepan over medium heat. Stir in brown sugar, 2 tablespoons juice, and cinnamon; cook 3 minutes, stirring constantly. Pour brown sugar mixture into prepared pan. Sprinkle cranberry mixture evenly over brown sugar mixture.

2. Weigh or lightly spoon 6.75 ounces flour (about 1½ cups) into dry measuring cups; level with a knife. Combine flour, baking powder, and salt in a bowl, stirring well with a whisk. Place granulated sugar and remaining 6 tablespoons butter in a large bowl; beat with a mixer at medium speed until well blended. Add vanilla and egg; beat well. Add flour mixture and buttermilk alternately to granulated sugar mixture, beginning and ending with flour mixture. Spoon batter over cranberry mixture.

3. Bake at 350° for 40 minutes or until a wooden pick inserted in center comes out clean. Cool in pan 5 minutes on a wire rack; run a knife around outside edges. Invert cake onto a plate; cool.

4. To prepare glaze, combine powdered sugar and remaining ingredients in a small bowl, stirring until smooth. Drizzle over cake. **Serves 16 (serving size: 1 square).**

CALORIES 234; FAT 6.8g (sat 3.8g, mono 0.8g, poly 1.7g); PROTEIN 2.3g; CARB 41.8g; FIBER 1g; CHOL 29mg; IRON 0.9mg; SODIUM 177mg; CALC 24mg

■ **BAKING 101 TIP**

Coating the pan with cooking spray and dusting it with flour is an important step. If skipped, some of the beautiful topping may be left behind in the pan.

Breakfast Coffee Cake

1½ cups granulated sugar, divided
½ cup nutlike cereal nuggets
2 teaspoons instant espresso granules
1 teaspoon ground cinnamon
7.75 ounces all-purpose flour (about 1¾ cups)
1 teaspoon baking soda
½ teaspoon baking powder
½ teaspoon salt
1 cup vanilla fat-free yogurt (about 8 ounces)
½ cup butter, softened
4 large egg whites
Cooking spray
1½ cups powdered sugar, sifted
2 tablespoons cooled brewed coffee

1. Preheat oven to 350°. Combine ½ cup granulated sugar, cereal, espresso granules, and cinnamon in a small bowl, stirring with a whisk. Set aside.

2. Weigh or lightly spoon flour into dry measuring cups; level with a knife. Combine flour, remaining 1 cup granulated sugar, baking soda, baking powder, and salt in a large bowl. Add yogurt, butter, and egg whites; beat with a mixer at low speed 1 minute or until combined.

3. Spread half of batter into an 8-inch square glass or ceramic baking dish coated with cooking spray. Sprinkle with cereal mixture; top with remaining half of batter. Bake at 350° for 45 minutes or until a wooden pick inserted in center comes out clean; cool in pan.

4. Combine powdered sugar and coffee in a small bowl; drizzle glaze evenly over top of cake. **Serves 14 (serving size: 1 piece).**

CALORIES 275; FAT 6.8g (sat 4.2g, mono 1.7g, poly 0.3g); PROTEIN 3.9g; CARB 50.9g; FIBER 0.9g; CHOL 17mg; IRON 2.1mg; SODIUM 293mg; CALC 52mg

■ BAKING 101 TIP

This cake freezes nicely, but be sure to leave off the glaze before freezing. When you're ready to serve, thaw the cake, and then add the glaze.

QUICK BREAD LOAVES & COFFEE CAKES

Walnut Coffee Cake

¾ cup packed dark brown sugar	1½ cups granulated sugar
⅓ cup chopped walnuts	10 tablespoons butter, softened
1 teaspoon ground cinnamon	6 large egg whites
14.5 ounces all-purpose flour (about 3¼ cups)	1 teaspoon vanilla extract
2 teaspoons baking soda	1½ cups nonfat buttermilk
1 teaspoon baking powder	Cooking spray
¼ teaspoon salt	

1. Preheat oven to 350°. Combine first 3 ingredients in a small bowl. Set aside.

2. Weigh or lightly spoon flour into dry measuring cups; level with a knife. Combine flour and next 3 ingredients in a medium bowl, stirring well with a whisk. Combine granulated sugar and butter in a large bowl; beat with a mixer at medium-high speed until well combined (about 3 minutes). Add egg whites; beat 3 minutes or until combined. Beat in vanilla. Add flour mixture and buttermilk alternately to sugar mixture, beginning and ending with flour mixture, beating well after each addition and scraping sides of bowl.

3. Spoon half of batter into a 10-inch Bundt pan coated with cooking spray. Sprinkle half of brown sugar mixture evenly over batter; spoon remaining half of batter into pan. Top with remaining brown sugar mixture. Bake at 350° for 55 minutes or until a wooden pick inserted in center comes out clean. Cool in pan 10 minutes on a wire rack; remove from pan. Cool completely on wire rack. **Serves 16 (serving size: 1 slice).**

CALORIES 298; FAT 9g (sat 4.7g, mono 2.1g, poly 1.6g); PROTEIN 5.1g; CARB 50.3g; FIBER 0.9g; CHOL 19mg; IRON 1.7mg; SODIUM 326mg; CALC 68mg

■ BAKING 101 TIP

Inside this classic cake is a sweet streak of brown sugar and warm cinnamon with the nutty crunch of walnuts. Chop the walnuts to the size of small peas to ensure that they distribute evenly in the cake. Substitute pecans for the walnuts, if you'd like.

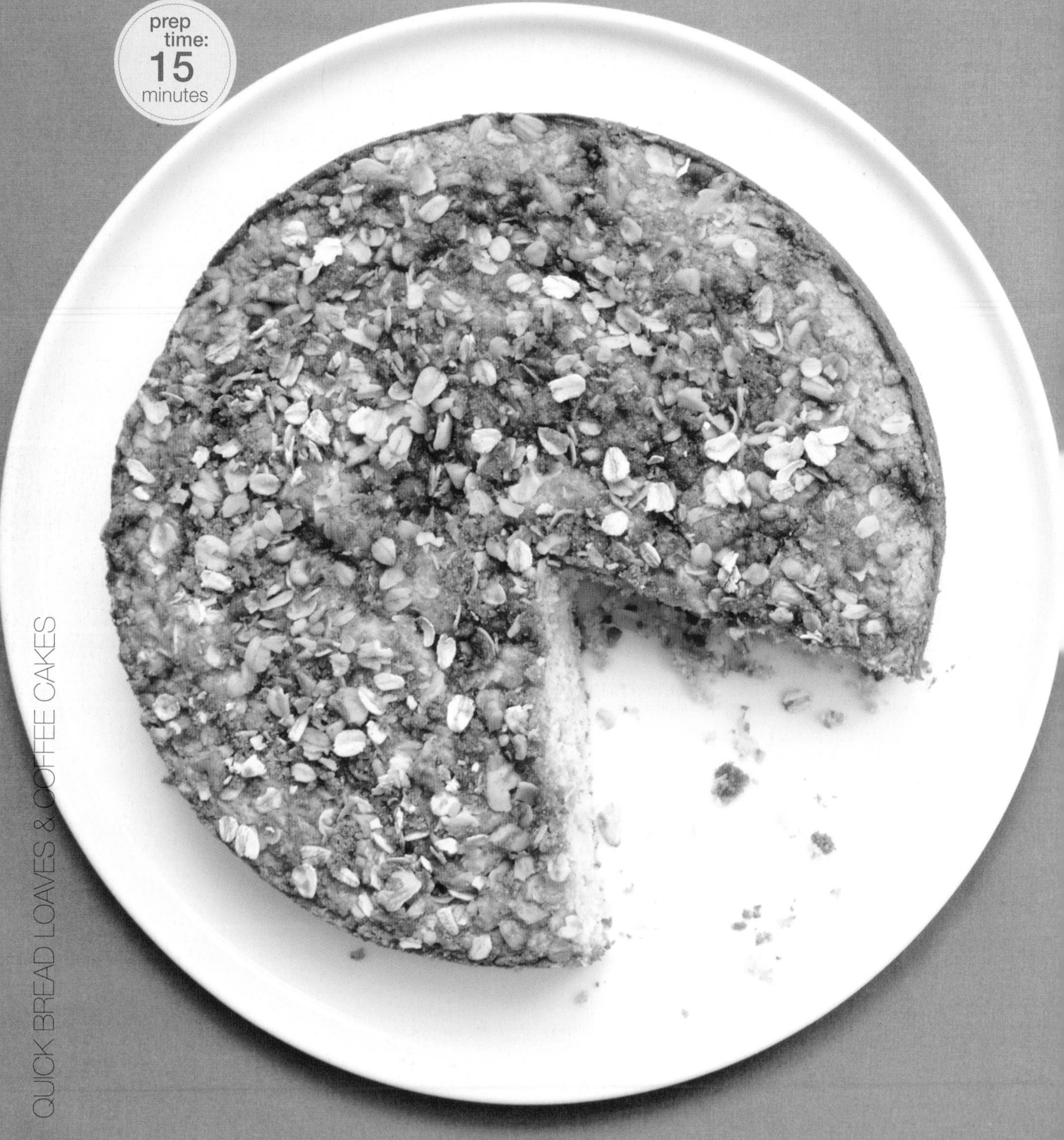

prep time: 15 minutes

Sour Cream Coffee Cake

- ¾ cup old-fashioned rolled oats (about 2.5 ounces), divided
- 4.5 ounces all-purpose flour (about 1 cup)
- 1 ounce whole-wheat flour (about ¼ cup)
- 1 teaspoon baking powder
- ½ teaspoon baking soda
- ¼ teaspoon salt
- ½ cup granulated sugar
- ½ cup packed brown sugar, divided
- ⅓ cup butter, softened
- 2 large eggs
- 1 teaspoon vanilla extract
- 1 (8-ounce) carton light sour cream
- Cooking spray
- 2 tablespoons finely chopped walnuts, toasted
- ½ teaspoon ground cinnamon
- 1 tablespoon chilled butter, cut into small pieces

1. Preheat oven to 350°. Spread oats in a single layer on a baking sheet. Bake at 350° for 6 minutes or until oats are slightly fragrant and light brown.

2. Set aside ¼ cup oats. Place remaining oats in a food processor; process 4 seconds or until finely ground. Weigh or lightly spoon flours into dry measuring cups; level with a knife. Combine flours, processed oats, baking powder, baking soda, and salt, stirring with a whisk.

3. Place granulated sugar, ¼ cup brown sugar, and ⅓ cup butter in a large bowl; beat with a mixer at medium speed 3 minutes or until light and fluffy. Add eggs, 1 at a time, beating well after each addition. Beat in vanilla. Add flour mixture to sugar mixture alternately with sour cream, beginning and ending with flour mixture. (Batter will be slightly lumpy because of oats.) Spoon batter into a 9-inch springform pan coated with cooking spray.

4. Combine reserved ¼ cup oats, remaining ¼ cup brown sugar, nuts, and cinnamon in a bowl. Cut in 1 tablespoon butter with a pastry blender or 2 knives until mixture resembles coarse meal. Sprinkle top of batter evenly with nut mixture. Bake at 350° for 38 minutes or until a wooden pick inserted in center comes out clean, top is golden, and cake begins to pull away from sides of pan. Cool cake in pan 10 minutes; remove from pan. **Serves 12 (serving size: 1 piece).**

CALORIES 230; FAT 9.6g (sat 5.4g, mono 2.1g, poly 1g); PROTEIN 4.6g; CARB 32.1g; FIBER 1.2g; CHOL 51mg; IRON 1.3mg; SODIUM 206mg; CALC 49mg

■ BAKING 101 TIP

This rich cake is tastiest warm from the oven, but leftovers are also delicious. Wrap the cake in foil or plastic wrap, or place it in a zip-top plastic bag to prevent it from drying out. Store it at room temperature for up to two days or in the refrigerator for up to one week.

Cookies

COOKIES

Caramel, Apple, and Oatmeal Cookies

6.75 ounces all-purpose flour (about 1½ cups)
1½ cups old-fashioned rolled oats
1 teaspoon baking powder
½ teaspoon baking soda
½ teaspoon salt
¾ cup granulated sugar
¾ cup packed brown sugar
6 tablespoons unsalted butter, softened
2 teaspoons vanilla extract
1 large egg
¾ cup finely chopped dried apple slices
¾ cup caramel bits or 16 small soft caramel candies, chopped

1. Preheat oven to 350°. Weigh or lightly spoon flour into dry measuring cups; level with a knife. Combine flour and next 4 ingredients in a bowl, stirring well. Place sugars and butter in a large bowl; beat with a mixer at medium speed until light and fluffy. Add vanilla and egg; beat well. Gradually add flour mixture; beat at low speed just until combined. Fold in apple and caramel bits.

2. Drop dough by 2 teaspoonfuls 2 inches apart onto baking sheets lined with parchment paper. Flatten balls slightly with hand. Bake at 350° for 9 minutes. Cool 3 minutes on pans. Remove cookies from pans; cool completely on wire racks. **Serves 48 (serving size: 1 cookie).**

CALORIES 83; FAT 2g (sat 1.1g, mono 0.5g, poly 0.3g); PROTEIN 1.1g; CARB 15.5g; FIBER 0.5g; CHOL 8mg; IRON 0.4mg; SODIUM 74mg; CALC 17mg

■ BAKING 101 TIP

Ensure even baking by dropping the same amount of dough for each cookie. Use a measuring spoon to scoop the dough, and then push it onto the baking sheet with your finger or another spoon. You can also use a cookie scoop, which looks like a small ice-cream scoop.

White Chocolate, Strawberry, and Oatmeal Cookies

3.3   ounces all-purpose flour (about ¾ cup)
  1   cup old-fashioned rolled oats
  ½   teaspoon baking soda
  ¼   teaspoon salt
  ¾   cup packed brown sugar
  ¼   cup butter, softened

  1   teaspoon vanilla extract
  1   large egg
  ¾   cup coarsely chopped dried strawberries
  ⅓   cup premium white chocolate chips
Cooking spray

1. Preheat oven to 350°. Weigh or lightly spoon flour into dry measuring cups; level with a knife. Combine flour and next 3 ingredients, stirring with a whisk. Place sugar and butter in bowl of a stand mixer; beat at medium speed until well blended (about 3 minutes). Add vanilla and egg; beat well. Gradually add flour mixture, beating until blended. Add strawberries and chips; beat at low speed just until blended.

2. Drop dough by tablespoonfuls 2 inches apart onto baking sheets coated with cooking spray. Bake at 350° for 12 minutes or until lightly browned. Remove from oven; cool 1 minute on pans. Remove cookies from pans; cool completely on wire racks. **Serves 24 (serving size: 1 cookie).**

CALORIES 98; FAT 3.3g (sat 2.1g, mono 0.6g, poly 0.2g); PROTEIN 1.2g; CARB 16g; FIBER 0.6g; CHOL 14mg; IRON 0.5mg; SODIUM 73mg; CALC 11mg

■ **BAKING 101 TIP**
Because the dough is heavy, we used a sturdy stand mixer. You can use a hand mixer to cream the butter and sugar, and then stir in the remaining ingredients by hand.

Triple-Fruit Cookies

⅔ cup packed brown sugar
⅓ cup butter, softened
¼ cup light-colored corn syrup
2 tablespoons fresh orange juice
1 teaspoon vanilla extract
1 large egg
6.75 ounces all-purpose flour (about 1½ cups)
½ teaspoon baking soda
½ teaspoon baking powder
½ teaspoon ground cinnamon
¼ teaspoon salt
¼ teaspoon ground allspice
¼ cup dried blueberries
¼ cup dried cranberries
¼ cup dried cherries
¼ cup flaked sweetened coconut

1. Preheat oven to 350°. Place sugar and butter in a medium bowl; beat with a mixer at medium speed until well blended (about 3 minutes). Add corn syrup and next 3 ingredients; beat until well combined (about 2 minutes).
2. Weigh or lightly spoon flour into dry measuring cups; level with a knife. Combine flour and next 5 ingredients. Add flour mixture to butter mixture; stir just until combined. Add blueberries and remaining ingredients; stir gently.
3. Drop dough by rounded teaspoonfuls 2 inches apart onto ungreased baking sheets. Bake at 350° for 8 minutes or until golden. Cool 1 minute on pans. Remove cookies from pans, and cool on wire racks. **Serves 24 (serving size: 2 cookies).**

CALORIES 108; FAT 3.1g (sat 1.8g, mono 0.7g, poly 0.6g); PROTEIN 1.2g; CARB 19g; FIBER 0.7g; CHOL 16mg; IRON 0.6mg; SODIUM 90mg; CALC 17mg

prep
time:
10
minutes

■ **BAKING 101 TIP**

There's no need to flatten the cookies; they'll spread
and flatten as they bake.

prep time: 15 minutes

Cherry-Pistachio Wedding Cookies

- 6 ounces cake flour (about 1½ cups)
- 3 ounces all-purpose flour (about ⅔ cup)
- 1¼ cups powdered sugar, divided
- 2 teaspoons cornstarch
- ¼ teaspoon salt
- ½ cup chilled butter, cut into small pieces
- 3 teaspoons ice water
- 1½ teaspoons vanilla extract
- ½ cup dried tart cherries
- ¼ cup finely chopped salted dry-roasted pistachios
- Cooking spray

1. Preheat oven to 350°. Weigh or lightly spoon flours into dry measuring cups; level with a knife. Place flours, ¾ cup powdered sugar, cornstarch, and salt in a food processor; pulse to combine. With food processor on, add butter through food chute a few pieces at a time; process 1 minute or until mixture is the texture of sand.

2. Combine 3 teaspoons ice water and vanilla in a small bowl. With food processor on, slowly add ice water mixture through food chute; process 1 minute or until well combined (mixture will remain crumbly). Add cherries and pistachios; pulse 10 times or just until combined.

3. Transfer mixture to a bowl (mixture will be crumbly). Gently press mixture into a level tablespoon; pack lightly. Turn out onto a baking sheet coated with cooking spray. Repeat with remaining dough to form 32 cookies. Bake at 350° for 15 minutes or just until bottoms are golden. Remove from oven; cool 10 minutes on pan.

4. Place remaining ½ cup powdered sugar in a large bowl. Add cooled cookies; toss gently to coat with powdered sugar. Transfer cookies to wax paper to cool completely. **Serves 32 (serving size: 1 cookie).**

CALORIES 86; FAT 3.4g (sat 1.9g, mono 1g, poly 0.3g); PROTEIN 1g; CARB 12.9g; FIBER 0.8g; CHOL 8mg; IRON 0.6mg; SODIUM 43mg; CALC 4mg

■ BAKING 101 TIP

The combination of tender cake flour and sturdy all-purpose flour produces delicate cookies. The dough will be crumbly after you've combined all the ingredients, but it will hold its shape once molded in a tablespoon measure and turned onto a baking sheet. You may need to add one to two additional teaspoons of ice water to the dough to achieve the right consistency.

Lemon-Cornmeal Cookies

5.6 ounces all-purpose flour (about 1¼ cups)
½ cup cornmeal
2 teaspoons baking powder
¼ teaspoon salt
½ cup sugar
¼ cup butter, softened
¼ cup canola oil
¼ cup light-colored corn syrup
2 teaspoons grated lemon rind
2 large egg whites
Cooking spray

1. Preheat oven to 350°. Weigh or lightly spoon flour into dry measuring cups; level with a knife. Combine flour and next 3 ingredients in a medium bowl, stirring with a whisk. Place sugar and butter in a large bowl; beat with a mixer at medium speed until well blended (about 2 minutes). Add oil, syrup, rind, and egg whites, beating until blended. Gradually add flour mixture to sugar mixture; beat just until moist.

2. Drop dough by level tablespoonfuls 1 inch apart on 2 baking sheets coated with cooking spray. Bake at 350° for 9 minutes or until edges are golden. Place baking sheets on wire racks; cool completely. **Serves 24 (serving size: 1 cookie).**

CALORIES 96; FAT 4.3g (sat 1.4g, mono 1.9g, poly 0.8g); PROTEIN 1.2g; CARB 13.6g; FIBER 0.4g; CHOL 5mg; IRON 0.5mg; SODIUM 85mg; CALC 24mg

■ BAKING 101 TIP

Cornmeal lends a pleasant crunch to these citrusy cookies. For variety, substitute tangerine, orange, or lime rind.

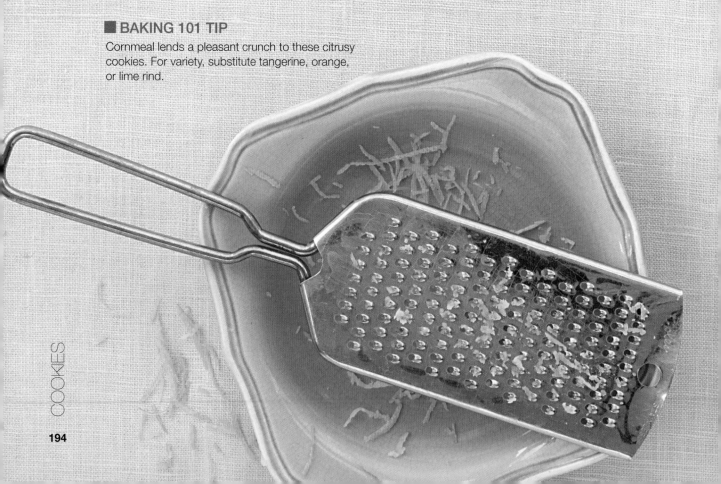

COOKIES

prep
time:
10
minutes

Amaretti

1 cup granulated sugar	2 large egg whites
1 (7-ounce) package almond paste	¼ cup turbinado sugar
1 teaspoon amaretto (almond-flavored liqueur)	

1. Preheat oven to 350°. Place granulated sugar and almond paste in a large bowl; beat with a mixer at medium speed until almond paste is broken into small pieces. Add amaretto and egg whites; beat at high speed 4 minutes or until smooth. Chill dough 20 minutes.

2. Drop dough by teaspoonfuls 1 inch apart onto baking sheets lined with parchment paper. Sprinkle evenly with turbinado sugar. Bake at 350° for 10 minutes or until edges of cookies are golden brown. Cool 5 minutes on pans. Carefully remove cookies from parchment, and cool on wire racks. **Serves 56 (serving size: 1 cookie).**

CALORIES 34; FAT 1g (sat 0.1g, mono 0.6g, poly 0.2g); PROTEIN 0.4g; CARB 6.1g; FIBER 0.1g; CHOL 0mg; IRON 0.1mg; SODIUM 2mg; CALC 6mg

■ BAKING 101 TIP

Lining pans with parchment paper prevents sticking, and you can reuse the paper for each batch.

Cinnamon Cookies

- **6** tablespoons granulated sugar
- **⅓** cup butter, softened
- **2** tablespoons brown sugar
- **2** teaspoons vanilla extract
- **2** large egg whites
- **6.75** ounces all-purpose flour (about 1½ cups)
- **¼** cup cornstarch
- **½** teaspoon baking powder
- **¼** teaspoon baking soda
- **¼** teaspoon salt
- **¼** teaspoon ground cinnamon
- **⅔** cup powdered sugar
- **2** teaspoons fat-free milk
- **⅛** teaspoon ground cinnamon
- **2** tablespoons sliced almonds

1. Preheat oven to 375°. Place first 4 ingredients in a large bowl; beat with a mixer at medium speed until well blended (about 5 minutes). Add egg whites, 1 at a time, beating well after each addition.

2. Weigh or lightly spoon flour into dry measuring cups; level with a knife. Combine flour and next 5 ingredients, stirring well with a whisk. Add to butter mixture; beat just until moist. Divide dough into 4 equal portions. Roll each portion to a ⅛-inch thickness between 2 sheets of plastic wrap. Freeze dough 20 minutes or until plastic wrap can be easily removed.

3. Working with 1 portion of dough at a time (keep remaining dough in freezer), remove top sheet of plastic wrap. Cut dough with a 2-inch round cookie cutter; place cookies onto ungreased baking sheets. Discard bottom sheet of plastic wrap. Repeat procedure with remaining dough. Bake at 375° for 8 minutes or until lightly browned. Remove from pans; cool on wire racks. Combine powdered sugar, milk, and ⅛ teaspoon cinnamon; drizzle mixture over cookies. Sprinkle with almonds. **Serves 28 (serving size: 1 cookie).**

CALORIES 77; FAT 2.4g (sat 1.4g, mono 0.7g, poly 0.2g); PROTEIN 1g; CARB 12.9g; FIBER 0.3g; CHOL 5mg; IRON 0.3mg; SODIUM 67mg; CALC 10mg

■ BAKING 101 TIP

Dip the cookie cutters in flour or powdered sugar to make clean cuts and prevent them from sticking to the dough.

prep
time:
10
minutes

Snickerdoodles

¾ **cup granulated sugar**
⅔ **cup brown sugar**
½ **cup butter, softened**
1 **teaspoon vanilla extract**
1 **large egg**
6.75 **ounces all-purpose flour (about 1½ cups)**

1 **teaspoon baking powder**
½ **teaspoon ground cinnamon**
¼ **teaspoon salt**
⅓ **cup granulated sugar**
1½ **teaspoons ground cinnamon**
Cooking spray

1. Preheat oven to 400°. Combine ¾ cup granulated sugar, brown sugar, and butter in a medium bowl; beat with a mixer at medium speed until well blended. Beat in vanilla and egg.

2. Weigh or lightly spoon flour into dry measuring cups; level with a knife. Combine flour and next 3 ingredients, stirring well with a whisk. Add flour mixture to butter mixture; beat just until combined. Shape dough into 30 balls.

3. Combine ⅓ cup granulated sugar and 1½ teaspoons cinnamon in a small shallow dish. Roll balls in sugar mixture, and place 2 inches apart on baking sheets coated with cooking spray. Bake at 400° for 8 minutes or until edges of cookies are golden brown. Cool 1 minute on pans. Remove cookies from pans, and cool on wire racks. **Serves 30 (serving size: 1 cookie).**

CALORIES 99; FAT 3.3g (sat 2g, mono 0.9g, poly 0.2g); PROTEIN 0.9g; CARB 16.9g; FIBER 0.3g; CHOL 15mg; IRON 0.5mg; SODIUM 59mg; CALC 17mg

■ BAKING 101 TIP

Be sure to use real butter, not margarine, which contains some water and will alter the texture of the cookies.

PLANT NO. 06-06
BUTTER
NET WT. 4 OZ. (113.4g)

prep
time:
15
minutes

prep
time:
17
minutes

Peanut Butter Cookies

1 cup granulated sugar
1 cup packed brown sugar
½ cup creamy peanut butter
¼ cup water
¼ cup canola oil
2 teaspoons vanilla extract

2 large egg whites
1 large egg
12 ounces all-purpose flour (about 2⅔ cups)
1 teaspoon baking powder
1 teaspoon baking soda
½ teaspoon salt

1. Preheat oven to 350°. Combine first 8 ingredients in a large bowl; beat with a mixer at medium speed until smooth.
2. Weigh or lightly spoon flour into dry measuring cups; level with a knife. Combine flour and next 3 ingredients in a small bowl, stirring with a whisk. Add flour mixture to peanut butter mixture, stirring just until combined.
3. Drop dough by tablespoonfuls 2 inches apart on 2 ungreased baking sheets. Bake at 350° for 12 minutes or until golden. Cool 2 minutes on pans. Remove from pans; cool on wire racks. **Serves 36 (serving size: 1 cookie).**

CALORIES 118; FAT 3.6g (sat 0.6g, mono 1.9g, poly 1g); PROTEIN 2.3g; CARB 19.6g; FIBER 0.5g; CHOL 6mg; IRON 0.6mg; SODIUM 102mg; CALC 16mg

■ BAKING 101 TIP

Don't overmix the dough once the dry ingredients are added, as doing so may result in tough cookies or ones that just don't rise well. Mix just until the ingredients are combined.

Chocolate Chip Cookies

10 ounces all-purpose flour (about 2¼ cups)	½ cup butter, softened
1 teaspoon baking soda	1 teaspoon vanilla extract
¼ teaspoon salt	2 large egg whites
1 cup packed brown sugar	¾ cup semisweet chocolate chips
¾ cup granulated sugar	Cooking spray

1. Preheat oven to 350°. Weigh or lightly spoon flour into dry measuring cups; level with a knife. Combine flour, baking soda, and salt, stirring with a whisk. Place sugars and butter in a large bowl; beat with a mixer at medium speed until well blended. Add vanilla and egg whites; beat 1 minute. Add flour mixture and chips; beat just until moist.

2. Drop dough by level tablespoonfuls 2 inches apart onto baking sheets coated with cooking spray. Bake at 350° for 10 minutes or until lightly browned. Cool 2 minutes on pans. Remove from pans; cool completely on wire racks.

Serves 40 (serving size: 1 cookie).

CALORIES 106; FAT 3.6g (sat 2.2g, mono 0.6g, poly 0.1g); PROTEIN 1.2g; CARB 17.5g; FIBER 0.2g; CHOL 6mg; IRON 0.5mg; SODIUM 67mg; CALC 6mg

■ BAKING 101 TIP

After baking, allow the cookies to stay on the pans for a couple minutes before transferring them to cooling racks; trying to move them too soon can result in broken cookies.

prep
time:
10
minutes

205

prep
time:
10
minutes

Toasted Coconut–Chocolate Chunk Cookies

1 cup flaked sweetened coconut
4.5 ounces all-purpose flour (about 1 cup)
½ teaspoon baking powder
¼ teaspoon baking soda
⅛ teaspoon salt
¾ cup packed brown sugar
¼ cup unsalted butter, softened
1 teaspoon vanilla extract
1 large egg
2 ounces dark chocolate (70% cacao), chopped
Cooking spray

1. Preheat oven to 350°. Arrange coconut in a single layer in a small metal baking pan. Bake at 350° for 7 minutes or until lightly toasted, stirring once. Set aside to cool.

2. Weigh or lightly spoon flour into a dry measuring cup; level with a knife. Combine flour and next 3 ingredients in a medium bowl, stirring with a whisk until blended. Place sugar and butter in a large bowl; beat with a mixer at medium speed until well blended. Beat in vanilla and egg. Add flour mixture, beating at low speed just until combined. Stir in toasted coconut and chocolate.

3. Drop dough by level tablespoonfuls 2 inches apart onto baking sheets coated with cooking spray. Bake at 350° for 10 minutes or until bottoms of cookies just begin to brown. Remove from pans, and cool completely on wire racks. **Serves 25 (serving size: 1 cookie).**

CALORIES 88; FAT 3.8g (sat 2.5g, mono 0.6g, poly 0.1g); PROTEIN 1g; CHOL 12mg; FIBER 0.4g; CARB 13g; IRON 0.6mg; SODIUM 38mg; CALC 15mg

■ BAKING 101 TIP

Always place dough on cool baking sheets because warm or hot pans will cause the cookies to spread. If you have only one baking sheet, you can quickly cool it by placing it under cold running water. Dry it thoroughly before arranging the dough on the pan.

prep
time:
10
minutes

■ BAKING 101 TIP

The ever-popular chocolate chip cookie gets
a delicious face lift with the addition of cocoa
powder and sweet-tart dried cherries.

Chewy Chocolate-Cherry Cookies

4.5 ounces all-purpose flour (about 1 cup)
⅓ cup unsweetened cocoa
½ teaspoon baking powder
¼ teaspoon baking soda
¼ teaspoon salt
1 cup sugar
⅓ cup butter, softened
1 teaspoon vanilla extract
1 large egg
⅔ cup dried tart cherries
3 tablespoons semisweet chocolate chips
Cooking spray

1. Preheat oven to 350°. Weigh or lightly spoon flour into a dry measuring cup; level with a knife. Combine flour and next 4 ingredients, stirring with a whisk. Place sugar and butter in a large bowl; beat with a mixer at high speed until well blended. Add vanilla and egg; beat well. With mixer at low speed, gradually add flour mixture; beat just until combined. Stir in cherries and chocolate chips.

2. Drop dough by tablespoonfuls 2 inches apart onto baking sheets coated with cooking spray. Bake at 350° for 12 minutes or just until set. Remove from oven; cool on pans 5 minutes. Remove from pans; cool completely on wire racks. **Serves 30 (serving size: 1 cookie).**

CALORIES 80; FAT 2.7g (sat 1.3g, mono 1.1g, poly 0.1g); PROTEIN 1.1g; CARB 13.4g; FIBER 0.8g; CHOL 12mg; IRON 0.4mg; SODIUM 56mg; CALC 10mg

Mexican Chocolate Cookies

5 ounces bittersweet chocolate, coarsely chopped

3.3 ounces all-purpose flour (about ¾ cup)

½ teaspoon ground cinnamon

¼ teaspoon baking powder

¼ teaspoon salt

Dash of freshly ground black pepper

Dash of ground red pepper

1¼ cups sugar

¼ cup butter, softened

1 large egg

1 teaspoon vanilla extract

Cooking spray

1. Preheat oven to 350°. Place chocolate in a small microwave-safe bowl; microwave at HIGH 1 minute or until almost melted, stirring until smooth. Cool to room temperature.

2. Weigh or lightly spoon flour into dry measuring cups; level with a knife. Combine flour and next 5 ingredients, stirring with a whisk. Place sugar and butter in a large bowl; beat with a mixer at medium speed until well blended (about 5 minutes). Add egg; beat well. Add cooled chocolate and vanilla; beat just until blended. Add flour mixture; beat just until moist.

3. Drop dough by level tablespoons 2 inches apart onto baking sheets coated with cooking spray. Bake at 350° for 10 minutes or until almost set. Remove from oven. Cool 2 minutes on pans or until set. Remove from pans; cool completely on wire racks. **Serves 32 (serving size: 1 cookie).**

CALORIES 80; FAT 2.9g (sat 1.7g, mono 0.6g, poly 0.1g); PROTEIN 0.7g; CARB 12.8g; FIBER 0.1g; CHOL 10mg; IRON 0.2mg; SODIUM 35mg; CALC 4mg

■ BAKING 101 TIP

The bittersweet chocolate in these cookies mellows the heat of the ground red pepper. You can use semisweet chocolate in place of the bittersweet, if you like.

COOKIES

Crunchy Sesame Cookies

6.75 ounces all-purpose flour (about 1½ cups)
1½ tablespoons cornstarch
1 teaspoon baking powder
½ teaspoon baking soda
¼ teaspoon salt
1 cup packed brown sugar
⅓ cup tahini (roasted sesame seed paste)

2 tablespoons dark sesame oil
1 tablespoon light-colored corn syrup
2 teaspoons vanilla extract
1 large egg
Cooking spray
2 tablespoons granulated sugar
1 tablespoon sesame seeds, toasted

1. Preheat oven to 375°. Weigh or lightly spoon flour into dry measuring cups; level with a knife. Combine flour and next 4 ingredients, stirring with a whisk. Place brown sugar, tahini, and oil in a large bowl; beat with a mixer at medium speed until well blended. Add syrup, vanilla, and egg; beat well. Gradually add flour mixture to sugar mixture, beating at low speed just until combined.

2. Lightly coat hands with cooking spray. Shape dough into 36 balls (about 1 inch each). Place granulated sugar in a shallow bowl. Roll dough balls in granulated sugar; place 2 inches apart on baking sheets lined with parchment paper. Flatten balls slightly with the bottom of a glass. Lightly spray tops of cookies with cooking spray; sprinkle sesame seeds evenly over cookies, pressing lightly to adhere. Bake at 375° for 10 minutes or until lightly browned. Cool 2 minutes on pans. Remove cookies from pans; cool completely on wire racks. **Serves 36 (serving size: 1 cookie).**

CALORIES 72; FAT 2.3g (sat 0.3g, mono 0.8g, poly 0.9g); PROTEIN 1.2g; CARB 12g; FIBER 0.3g; CHOL 6mg; IRON 0.8mg; SODIUM 50mg; CALC 17mg

■ **BAKING 101 TIP**

Tahini (roasted sesame seed paste) and dark sesame oil deliver nuanced bittersweet sesame flavor. A touch of cornstarch ensures crispness.

prep
time:
20
minutes

213

Macadamia Butter Cookies with Dried Cranberries

⅔ cup macadamia nuts
½ cup granulated sugar
½ cup packed brown sugar
1 teaspoon vanilla extract
1 large egg
5.5 ounces all-purpose flour (about 1¼ cups)

½ teaspoon baking soda
¼ teaspoon salt
⅛ teaspoon ground nutmeg
½ cup sweetened dried cranberries, chopped
¼ cup granulated sugar

1. Preheat oven to 375°. Place nuts in a food processor; process until smooth (about 2 minutes), scraping sides of bowl once. Combine ground nuts, ½ cup granulated sugar, and brown sugar in a large bowl; beat with a mixer at medium speed. Add vanilla and egg; beat well.

2. Weigh or lightly spoon flour into dry measuring cups; level with a knife. Combine flour and next 3 ingredients, stirring with a whisk. Add flour mixture to sugar mixture; beat at low speed just until combined (mixture will be very thick). Stir in cranberries. Chill 10 minutes.

3. Divide chilled dough into 30 equal portions; roll each portion into a ball. Place ¼ cup granulated sugar in a shallow dish; lightly press each ball into sugar. Place each ball, sugar side up, on a baking sheet lined with parchment paper. Bake cookies, 1 baking sheet at a time, at 375° for 9 minutes or until golden. Remove cookies from pan; cool on a wire rack. **Serves 30 (serving size: 1 cookie).**

CALORIES 76; FAT 2.5g (sat 0.4g, mono 1.8g, poly 0.1g); PROTEIN 1g; CARB 13.2g; FIBER 0.6g; CHOL 7mg; IRON 0.5mg; SODIUM 44mg; CALC 7mg

■ **BAKING 101 TIP**

The dough is somewhat sticky; chilling it briefly makes handling easier and helps the cookies hold a nice shape as they bake. The dough balls just need a very light coating of sugar. Discard the leftover sugar.

COOKIES

Raspberry Thumbprint Cookies

¾ cup (3 ounces) grated almond paste	1 large egg white
⅔ cup sugar	5.5 ounces all-purpose flour (about 1¼ cups)
5 tablespoons butter, softened	¼ teaspoon salt
¼ teaspoon vanilla extract	6 tablespoons seedless raspberry jam

1. Preheat oven to 325°. Line 2 large baking sheets with parchment paper.

2. Place first 3 ingredients in a bowl; beat with a mixer at medium speed 4 minutes or until light and fluffy. Add vanilla and egg white; beat well.

3. Weigh or lightly spoon flour into dry measuring cups; level with a knife. Add flour and salt to almond paste mixture; beat at low speed until well blended. Turn dough out onto a lightly floured surface, and shape dough into 36 (1-inch) balls. Place balls 1 inch apart on prepared baking sheets, and press thumb into center of each cookie, leaving an indentation. Bake at 325° for 10 minutes or until golden. Remove cookies from pans; cool on wire racks. Spoon about ½ teaspoon jam into center of each cookie. **Serves 36 (serving size: 1 cookie).**

CALORIES 61; FAT 2.3g (sat 1.1g, mono 0.8g, poly 0.2g); PROTEIN 0.8g; CARB 9.5g; FIBER 0.4g; CHOL 4mg; IRON 0.3mg; SODIUM 29mg; CALC 6mg

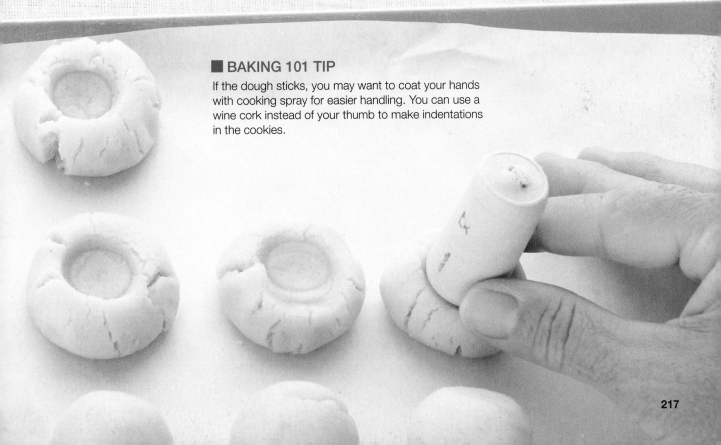

■ BAKING 101 TIP

If the dough sticks, you may want to coat your hands with cooking spray for easier handling. You can use a wine cork instead of your thumb to make indentations in the cookies.

COOKIES

Ginger Cookies

6 tablespoons butter, softened
⅔ cup plus 3 tablespoons sugar, divided
¼ cup molasses
1 large egg
9 ounces all-purpose flour (about 2 cups)

2 teaspoons baking soda
1 teaspoon ground ginger
1 teaspoon ground cinnamon
½ teaspoon ground mace
Cooking spray

1. Place butter in a large bowl; beat with a mixer at medium speed until fluffy. Gradually add ⅔ cup sugar, beating at medium speed until well blended. Add molasses and egg; beat well.

2. Weigh or lightly spoon flour into dry measuring cups; level with a knife. Combine flour and next 4 ingredients, stirring with a whisk. Gradually add flour mixture to butter mixture, stirring until blended. Divide dough in half. Wrap each portion in plastic wrap, and freeze 30 minutes.

3. Preheat oven to 350°. Shape each portion of dough into 20 (1-inch) balls. Place remaining 3 tablespoons sugar in a shallow dish; roll dough balls in sugar. Place dough balls 2 inches apart on baking sheets coated with cooking spray. Flatten cookies with bottom of a glass to a ½-inch thickness. Bake at 350° for 12 minutes or until lightly browned. Remove from pans, and cool completely on wire racks. **Serves 40 (serving size: 1 cookie).**

CALORIES 62; FAT 2g (sat 1.2g, mono 0.5g, poly 0.1g); PROTEIN 0.8g; CARB 10.7g; FIBER 0.3g; CHOL 10mg; IRON 0.4mg; SODIUM 78mg; CALC 8mg

■ **BAKING 101 TIP**
If the dough starts to stick to the bottom of the glass you use for flattening, coat the glass with cooking spray after every three or four cookies.

Brown Sugar–Pecan Shortbread

6.75 **ounces all-purpose flour (about 1½ cups)**
 ¼ **cup cornstarch**
 3 **tablespoons finely chopped pecans, toasted**
 ⅛ **teaspoon salt**
 ½ **cup packed dark brown sugar**
 ½ **cup butter, softened**
 ¼ **cup ice water**
 2 **tablespoons turbinado sugar**

1. Weigh or lightly spoon flour into dry measuring cups; level with a knife. Combine flour and next 3 ingredients, stirring well with a whisk. Place brown sugar and butter in a medium bowl; beat with a mixer at medium speed until light and fluffy (about 1 minute). Gradually add flour mixture, beating at low speed (mixture will appear crumbly). Sprinkle ¼ cup ice water over flour mixture; beat at low speed just until combined. Shape dough into 2 (6-inch-long) logs; wrap each log in plastic wrap. Chill 1 hour or until very firm.

2. Preheat oven to 350°. Line baking sheets with parchment paper.

3. Unwrap dough; cut each log into 16 slices. Place dough circles 1 inch apart on prepared baking sheets. Sprinkle tops evenly with turbinado sugar, gently pressing into dough. Bake at 350° for 18 minutes or until lightly browned. Remove from pans; cool on wire racks. **Serves 32 (serving size: 1 cookie).**

CALORIES 70; FAT 3.4g (sat 1.9g, mono 1g, poly 0.3g); PROTEIN 0.7g; CARB 9.4g; FIBER 0.2g; CHOL 8mg; IRON 0.4mg; SODIUM 31mg; CALC 5mg

■ BAKING 101 TIP

If you don't want to bake all the cookies at once, freeze one dough log for up to two months. Slice the frozen dough, and bake; if the dough is too hard to slice, let it stand at room temperature for 10 to 15 minutes.

prep
time:
12
minutes

■ **BAKING 101 TIP**

A combination of cardamom, cinnamon, cloves, and
black pepper gives these cookies a taste reminiscent
of Indian spiced tea. Using powdered sugar helps them
retain the characteristic shortbread crunch.

Chai Shortbread

6.75 ounces all-purpose flour (about 1½ cups)	**Dash** of freshly ground black pepper
⅛ teaspoon salt	**¾** cup powdered sugar
⅛ teaspoon ground cardamom	**10** tablespoons butter, softened
⅛ teaspoon ground cinnamon	**1** tablespoon ice water
Dash of ground cloves	

1. Weigh or lightly spoon flour into dry measuring cups; level with a knife. Combine flour and next 5 ingredients, stirring well with a whisk. Place sugar and butter in a medium bowl; beat with a mixer at medium speed until light and fluffy. Gradually add flour mixture to butter mixture, beating at low speed just until combined (mixture will appear crumbly). Sprinkle dough with 1 tablespoon ice water; toss with a fork. Divide dough in half. Shape dough into 2 (6-inch-long) logs; wrap each log in plastic wrap. Chill 1 hour or until very firm.

2. Preheat oven to 375°. Unwrap dough logs. Carefully cut each log into 18 slices. Place dough circles 2 inches apart on baking sheets lined with parchment paper. Bake at 375° for 10 minutes. Cool 5 minutes on pans. Remove cookies from pans; cool completely on wire racks. **Serves 36 (serving size: 1 cookie).**

CALORIES 57; FAT 3.2g (sat 2g, mono 0.8g, poly 0.1g); PROTEIN 0.6g; CARB 6.5g; FIBER 0.2g; CHOL 8mg; IRON 0.3mg; SODIUM 31mg; CALC 2mg

Bars &
Squares

Apple-Walnut Bars

3 ounces all-purpose flour (about ⅔ cup)
2 teaspoons baking powder
½ teaspoon salt
1 cup packed brown sugar
1 teaspoon vanilla extract
2 large eggs

2 cups diced peeled apple
½ cup coarsely chopped walnuts (about 2 ounces)
⅓ cup raisins
Cooking spray

1. Preheat oven to 350°. Weigh or lightly spoon flour into a dry measuring cup; level with a knife. Combine flour, baking powder, and salt, stirring with a wisk. Combine sugar, vanilla, and eggs in a medium bowl, and beat with a mixer at medium speed until sugar dissolves. Add flour mixture to egg mixture; stir until blended. Stir in apple, walnuts, and raisins.

2. Spoon batter into an 8-inch square glass or ceramic baking dish coated with cooking spray. Bake at 350° for 40 minutes or until golden brown and a wooden pick inserted in center comes out clean. Cool in pan on a wire rack.

Serves 9 (serving size: 1 bar).

CALORIES 218; FAT 5.6g (sat 0.8g, mono 1g, poly 3.4g); PROTEIN 3.6g; CARB 40.2g; FIBER 1.3g; CHOL 47mg; IRON 1.5mg; SODIUM 266mg; CALC 99mg

■ BAKING 101 TIP

Set your timer for three to five minutes before the time specified in the recipe. That way, if your oven runs hot, you can remove the bars before they overcook.

Apricot Cobbler Bars

  5 tablespoons butter, softened
  ¼ cup powdered sugar
  ¼ cup packed brown sugar
  ¼ teaspoon salt
  ⅛ teaspoon almond extract
  5.6 ounces all-purpose flour (about 1¼ cups)
  ¾ cup apricot preserves
  ½ cup low-fat granola without raisins, crushed

1. Preheat oven to 350°. Beat butter with a mixer at medium speed until light and fluffy. Add sugars, salt, and almond extract, beating well. Weigh or lightly spoon flour into dry measuring cups; level with a knife. Gradually add flour to butter mixture, beating until moist. Remove ⅓ cup flour mixture, and set aside.

2. Press remaining flour mixture into bottom of an 8-inch square glass or ceramic baking dish. Bake at 350° for 15 minutes or until lightly golden. Gently spread preserves over warm shortbread. Combine reserved ⅓ cup flour mixture and granola; sprinkle over preserves. Bake an additional 20 minutes or until golden brown. Cool in pan on a wire rack. **Serves 24 (serving size: 1 bar).**

CALORIES 91; FAT 2.6g (sat 1.5g, mono 0.8g, poly 0.1g); PROTEIN 0.9g; CARB 16.5g; FIBER 0.4g; CHOL 6mg; IRON 0.5mg; SODIUM 59mg; CALC 7mg

■ BAKING 101 TIP

These bar cookies can be made several days in advance; store them in an airtight container with wax paper between layers to prevent sticking.

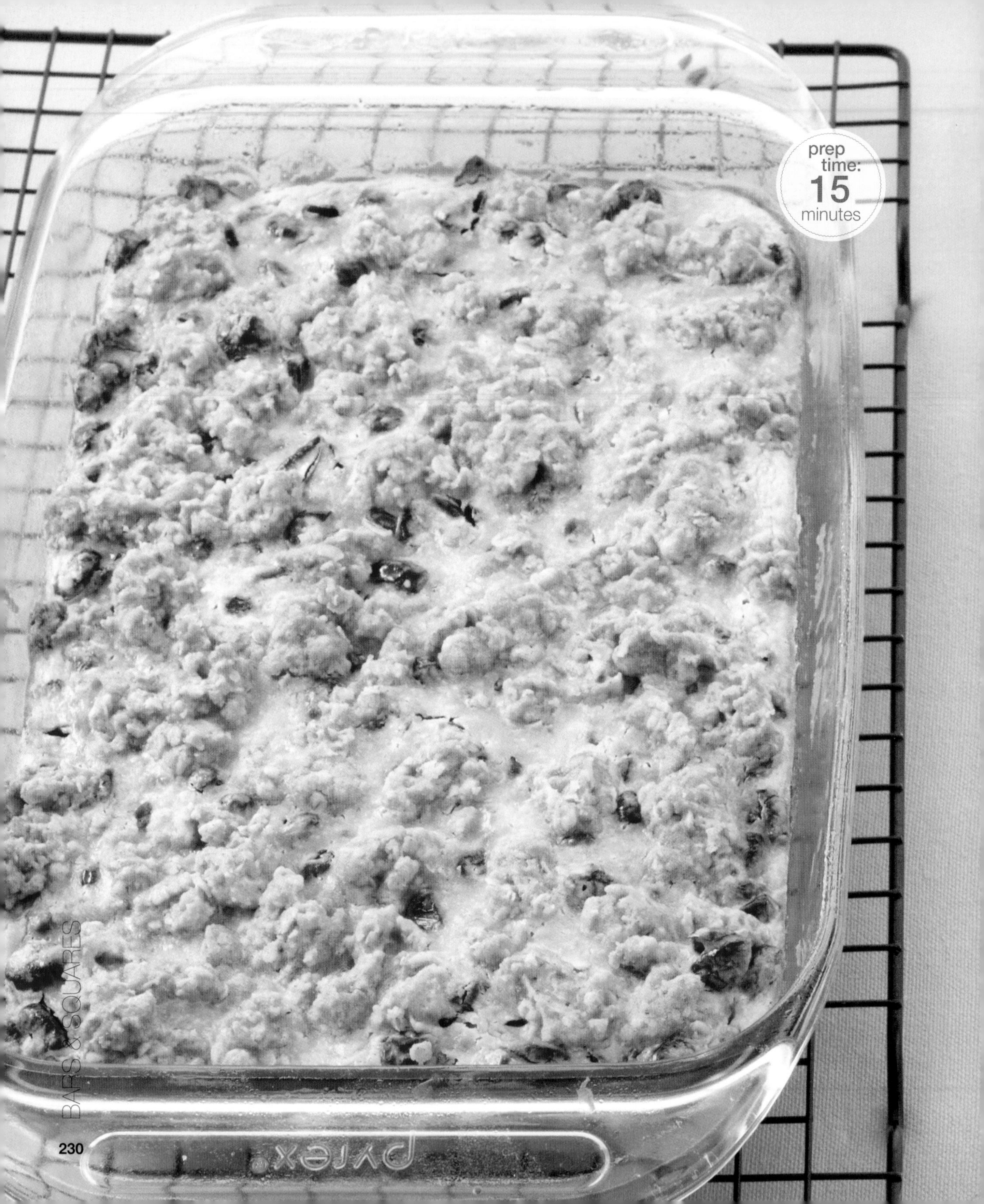

prep time: 15 minutes

Cranberry-Oatmeal Bars

Crust:
- 4.5 ounces all-purpose flour (about 1 cup)
- 1 cup quick-cooking oats
- ½ cup packed brown sugar
- ¼ teaspoon salt
- ¼ teaspoon baking soda
- ¼ teaspoon ground cinnamon
- 6 tablespoons butter, melted
- 3 tablespoons fresh orange juice
- Cooking spray

Filling:
- 1⅓ cups dried cranberries (about 6 ounces)
- ¾ cup sour cream
- ½ cup granulated sugar
- 2 tablespoons all-purpose flour
- 1 teaspoon vanilla extract
- ½ teaspoon grated orange rind
- 1 large egg white, lightly beaten

1. Preheat oven to 325°. To prepare crust, weigh or lightly spoon flour into a dry measuring cup; level with a knife. Combine flour and next 5 ingredients in a medium bowl, stirring well with a whisk. Drizzle butter and juice over flour mixture, stirring just until moist (mixture will be crumbly). Reserve ½ cup oat mixture. Press remaining oat mixture into bottom of an 11 x 7–inch glass or ceramic baking dish coated with cooking spray.

2. To prepare filling, combine cranberries and next 6 ingredients in a medium bowl, stirring well. Spread cranberry mixture over prepared crust; sprinkle reserved oat mixture evenly over filling. Bake at 325° for 40 minutes or until edges are golden. Cool completely in pan on a wire rack. **Serves 24 (serving size: 1 bar).**

CALORIES 133; FAT 4.6g (sat 2.6g, mono 0.8g, poly 0.2g); PROTEIN 1.5g; CARB 21.9g; FIBER 0.9g; CHOL 13mg; IRON 0.6mg; SODIUM 67mg; CALC 20mg

■ BAKING 101 TIP

Cooling the bars completely in the pan makes cutting them easier and cleaner. Substitute dried cherries or chopped dried apricots to vary the flavor of these bars.

Fig Bars

1 (8-ounce) package dried figs
½ cup port wine
½ cup fresh orange juice
4.5 ounces all-purpose flour (about 1 cup)
1½ cups quick-cooking oats
⅔ cup packed brown sugar
½ teaspoon ground cinnamon
6 tablespoons chilled butter, cut into pieces
1 large egg white
Cooking spray

1. Remove stems from figs; discard stems. Coarsely chop figs. Combine figs, wine, and juice in a medium saucepan; bring to a boil over medium heat. Reduce heat, and simmer, uncovered, until figs are tender and most of liquid is absorbed, stirring occasionally (about 20 minutes). Remove from heat. Cool slightly. Place fig mixture in a food processor; process until smooth. Spoon into a bowl; cool completely.
2. Preheat oven to 350°. Weigh or lightly spoon flour into a dry measuring cup; level with a knife. Place flour and next 3 ingredients in a food processor; process until oats are finely ground. Add butter; process until mixture resembles coarse meal. Add egg white; pulse to combine.
3. Firmly press half of crumb mixture into an 8-inch square metal baking pan coated with cooking spray. Spread fig mixture over crumb mixture. Sprinkle with remaining crumb mixture; press gently. Bake at 350° for 25 minutes. Cool completely in pan on a wire rack. **Serves 25 (serving size: 1 bar).**

CALORIES 112; FAT 3.2g (sat 1.5g, mono 1.2g, poly 0.3g); PROTEIN 1.7g; CARB 19.5g; FIBER 1.5g; CHOL 7mg; IRON 0.8mg; SODIUM 25mg; CALC 25mg

■ BAKING 101 TIP

You can substitute 1¾ cups of chopped fresh figs for the dried, if you like. Fresh figs have a short season—mid to late summer—and are incredibly delicate, with a shelf life of two days or less.

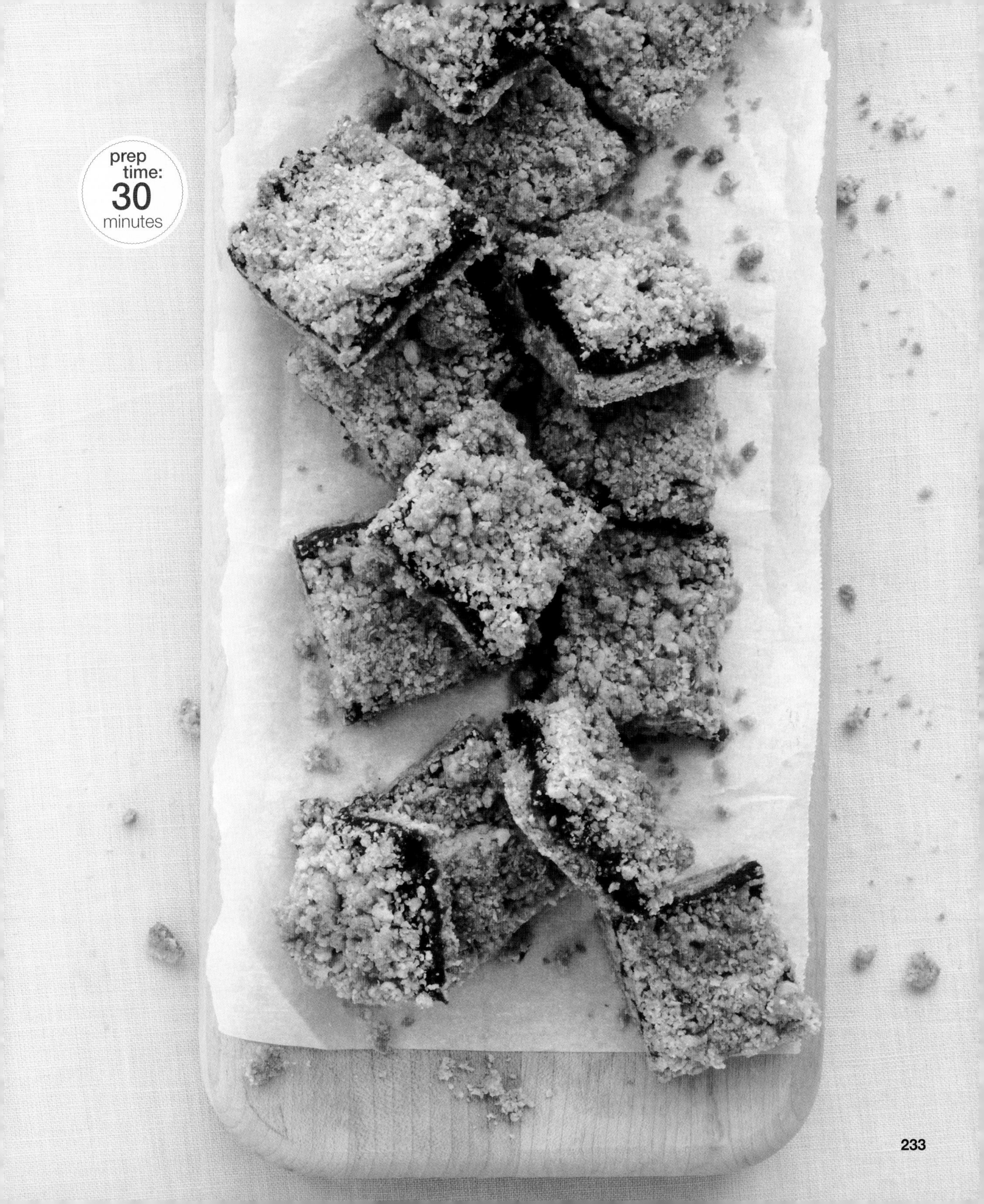

prep time:
30
minutes

prep
time:
10
minutes

Easy Lemon Squares

Crust:
- ¼ cup granulated sugar
- 3 tablespoons butter, softened
- 4.5 ounces all-purpose flour (about 1 cup)

Topping:
- 3 large eggs
- ¾ cup granulated sugar
- 2 teaspoons grated lemon rind
- ⅓ cup fresh lemon juice
- 3 tablespoons all-purpose flour
- ½ teaspoon baking powder
- ⅛ teaspoon salt
- 2 teaspoons powdered sugar

1. Preheat oven to 350°. To prepare crust, beat ¼ cup granulated sugar and butter with a mixer at medium speed until creamy. Weigh or lightly spoon 4.5 ounces flour (about 1 cup) into a dry measuring cup; level with a knife. Gradually add 4.5 ounces flour to sugar mixture, beating at low speed until mixture resembles coarse meal. Gently press mixture into bottom of an 8-inch square metal baking pan. Bake at 350° for 15 minutes; cool in pan on a wire rack.
2. To prepare topping, beat eggs at medium speed until foamy. Add ¾ cup granulated sugar and next 5 ingredients, and beat until well blended. Pour mixture over partially baked crust. Bake at 350° for 20 to 25 minutes or until set. Cool in pan on a wire rack. Sift powdered sugar evenly over top. **Serves 16 (serving size: 1 square).**

CALORIES 118; FAT 3.2g (sat 1.7g, mono 1g, poly 0.3g); PROTEIN 2.2g; CARB 20.5g; FIBER 0.3g; CHOL 47mg; IRON 0.6mg; SODIUM 68mg; CALC 16mg

■ **BAKING 101 TIP**

Be sure to zest the lemon before you squeeze the juice. One medium lemon yields about 1 teaspoon of grated rind and 2 to 3 tablespoons of juice, so you'll need two lemons to prepare this recipe.

BARS & SQUARES

prep
time:
20
minutes

Streusel-Topped Key Lime Squares

¼ cup butter, softened
¼ cup granulated sugar
1 teaspoon grated lime rind
⅛ teaspoon salt
⅛ teaspoon fresh lemon juice
4.5 ounces all-purpose flour (about 1 cup)
Cooking spray

⅔ cup granulated sugar
3 tablespoons all-purpose flour
¾ teaspoon baking powder
⅛ teaspoon salt
½ cup fresh Key lime juice
3 large eggs
1 tablespoon powdered sugar

1. Preheat oven to 350°. Place first 5 ingredients in a medium bowl; beat with a mixer at medium speed until creamy (about 2 minutes).

2. Weigh or lightly spoon 4.5 ounces flour (about 1 cup) into a dry measuring cup; level with a knife. Gradually add 4.5 ounces flour to butter mixture, beating at low speed until mixture resembles coarse meal. Gently press two-thirds of mixture (about 1⅓ cups) into bottom of an 8-inch square metal baking pan coated with cooking spray; set remaining ⅔ cup flour mixture aside. Bake at 350° for 12 minutes or until just beginning to brown.

3. Combine ⅔ cup granulated sugar, 3 tablespoons flour, baking powder, and ⅛ teaspoon salt in a medium bowl, stirring with a whisk. Add lime juice and eggs, stirring with a whisk until smooth. Pour mixture over partially baked crust. Bake at 350° for 12 minutes. Remove pan from oven (do not turn oven off); sprinkle reserved ⅔ cup flour mixture evenly over egg mixture. Bake an additional 8 to 10 minutes or until set. Remove from oven; cool in pan on a wire rack. Sprinkle evenly with powdered sugar. **Serves 16 (serving size: 1 square).**

CALORIES 121; FAT 3.9g (sat 1.7g, mono 1.5g, poly 0.3g); PROTEIN 2.2g; CARB 19.9g; FIBER 0.3g; CHOL 47mg; IRON 0.6mg; SODIUM 93mg; CALC 21mg

■ BAKING 101 TIP

If you can't find Key limes, you can use bottled Key lime juice. You can substitute regular Persian limes, but the squares won't be quite as tart.

Vanilla Bean Shortbread

Cooking spray
9 ounces all-purpose flour (about 2 cups)
¼ cup cornstarch
¼ teaspoon salt

½ cup butter, softened
½ cup canola oil
½ cup sugar
1 vanilla bean, split lengthwise

1. Preheat oven to 350°. Line bottom and sides of a 13 x 9–inch metal baking pan with foil; coat foil with cooking spray, and set aside.

2. Weigh or lightly spoon flour into dry measuring cups; level with a knife. Combine flour, cornstarch, and salt in a large bowl, stirring with a whisk. Place butter in a medium bowl; beat with a mixer at medium speed 2 minutes or until light and fluffy. Add oil; beat at medium speed 3 minutes or until well blended. Gradually add sugar, beating well. Scrape seeds from vanilla bean, and add seeds to butter mixture; discard bean. Add flour mixture, beating at low speed just until blended.

3. Spoon dough into prepared pan. Place a sheet of heavy-duty plastic wrap over dough; press to an even thickness. Discard plastic wrap. Bake at 350° for 30 minutes or until edges are lightly browned. Cool in pan 5 minutes on a wire rack. Carefully lift foil from pan; cool squares completely on wire rack. **Serves 32 (serving size: 1 square).**

CALORIES 101; FAT 6.4g (sat 2.1g, mono 2.8g, poly 1.2g); PROTEIN 0.9g; CARB 10.1g; FIBER 0.2g; CHOL 8mg; IRON 0.4mg; SODIUM 39mg; CALC 2mg

■ BAKING 101 TIP

Vanilla bean—as opposed to commercial extract—adds profound flavor. Extracting the pulp from the pod is simple. Just cut the bean in half lengthwise using a small knife, and scrape out the seeds with the knife blade.

Butterscotch Bars

1 cup packed brown sugar

5 tablespoons butter, melted

1 teaspoon vanilla extract

1 large egg, lightly beaten

9 ounces all-purpose flour (about 2 cups)

2½ cups quick-cooking oats

½ teaspoon salt

½ teaspoon baking soda

Cooking spray

1¼ cups butterscotch morsels (about 8 ounces)

¾ cup fat-free sweetened condensed milk

⅛ teaspoon salt

½ cup finely chopped walnuts, toasted

1. Preheat oven to 350°. Combine sugar and butter in a large bowl, and beat with a mixer at medium speed until blended. Stir in vanilla and egg. Weigh or lightly spoon flour into dry measuring cups; level with a knife. Combine flour and next 3 ingredients in a bowl. Add oat mixture to sugar mixture; stir with a fork until combined (mixture will be crumbly). Place 3 cups oat mixture in bottom of a 13 x 9–inch metal baking pan coated with cooking spray; press into bottom of pan. Set aside. Reserve remaining oat mixture.

2. Place butterscotch morsels, sweetened condensed milk, and ⅛ teaspoon salt in a microwave-safe bowl; microwave at HIGH 3 minutes or until butterscotch morsels melt, stirring every 20 seconds. Stir in walnuts. Scrape mixture into pan, spreading evenly over crust. Sprinkle evenly with remaining oat mixture, gently pressing into butterscotch mixture. Bake at 350° for 30 minutes or until topping is golden brown. Place pan on a wire rack; run a knife around outside edge. Cool completely. **Serves 36 (serving size: 1 bar).**

CALORIES 148; FAT 5.1g (sat 2.7g, mono 0.9g, poly 1.1g); PROTEIN 2.6g; CARB 23.4g; FIBER 0.8g; CHOL 11mg; IRON 0.8mg; SODIUM 87mg; CALC 31mg

■ BAKING 101 TIP

The flour and oats mixture is somewhat dry after combining, but it serves as both a solid base for the soft butterscotch layer and a crumbly, streusel-like topping.

BARS & SQUARES

Hello Dolly Bars

1½ cups graham cracker crumbs (about 9 cookie sheets)
2 tablespoons butter, melted
1 tablespoon water
⅓ cup semisweet chocolate chips
⅓ cup butterscotch morsels
⅔ cup flaked sweetened coconut
¼ cup chopped pecans, toasted
1 (15-ounce) can fat-free sweetened condensed milk

1. Preheat oven to 350°. Line bottom and sides of an 8-inch square metal baking pan with parchment paper; cut off excess parchment paper around top edge of pan.

2. Place crumbs in a medium bowl. Drizzle with butter and 1 tablespoon water; toss with a fork until moist. Gently pat mixture into an even layer in prepared pan (do not press firmly). Sprinkle chips and morsels over crumb mixture. Top evenly with coconut and pecans. Drizzle milk evenly over top. Bake at 350° for 25 minutes or until lightly browned and bubbly around edges. Cool completely in pan on a wire rack. **Serves 24 (serving size: 1 bar).**

CALORIES 123; FAT 4.4g (sat 2.3g, mono 1.3g, poly 0.6g); PROTEIN 2.1g; CARB 19.1g; FIBER 0.5g; CHOL 5mg; IRON 0.3mg; SODIUM 64mg; CALC 50mg

■ BAKING 101 TIP

The bars can create a sticky mess in the pan, so it's crucial to line it with parchment paper. Because the milk needs to seep into the graham cracker crumbs, don't pack the crumbs too tightly in the bottom of the pan.

Pecan-Date Bars

Crust:
  4.5 ounces all-purpose flour (about 1 cup)
  ⅓ cup packed brown sugar
  ¼ teaspoon salt
  ¼ cup chilled butter, cut into small pieces
  Cooking spray

Filling:
  ¾ cup dark corn syrup
  ⅓ cup packed brown sugar

  ¼ cup egg substitute
  2 tablespoons all-purpose flour
  1 tablespoon bourbon
  1 teaspoon vanilla extract
  ¼ teaspoon salt
  1 large egg
  ½ cup chopped pitted dates
  ⅓ cup chopped pecans, toasted
  2 tablespoons semisweet chocolate minichips

1. Preheat oven to 400°. To prepare crust, weigh or lightly spoon 4.5 ounces flour (about 1 cup) into a dry measuring cup; level with a knife. Combine 4.5 ounces flour, ⅓ cup sugar, and ¼ teaspoon salt, stirring well with a whisk. Cut in butter with a pastry blender or 2 knives until mixture resembles coarse meal. Press mixture into bottom of an 11 x 7–inch glass or ceramic baking dish coated with cooking spray. Bake at 400° for 12 minutes or until lightly browned. Cool completely.

2. Reduce oven temperature to 350°. To prepare filling, combine corn syrup and next 7 ingredients in a large bowl, stirring well with a whisk. Stir in dates, pecans, and chocolate chips. Pour mixture over prepared crust. Bake at 350° for 35 minutes or until set. Cool in pan on a wire rack. Cover and chill 1 hour or until firm. **Serves 24 (serving size: 1 bar).**

CALORIES 123; FAT 3.6g (sat 1.3g, mono 1.6g, poly 0.5g); PROTEIN 1.4g; CARB 22g; FIBER 0.7g; CHOL 14mg; IRON 0.6mg; SODIUM 89mg; CALC 13mg

■ BAKING 101 TIP

Use your fingers to press the crust mixture evenly and firmly into the bottom of the dish; a compact layer holds together when cut.

prep
time:
20
minutes

245

Fig and Cream Cheese Bars

6 ounces all-purpose flour (about 1⅓ cups)
¾ cup packed brown sugar
½ teaspoon salt
6 tablespoons chilled butter, cut into small pieces
   Cooking spray
2 cups dried figs, stems removed
1 cup water

½ cup granulated sugar, divided
3 tablespoons fresh lemon juice
¾ cup (6 ounces) ⅓-less-fat cream cheese, softened
1 teaspoon vanilla extract
1 large egg
2 teaspoons powdered sugar

1. Preheat oven to 350°. Weigh or lightly spoon flour into dry measuring cups; level with a knife. Combine flour, brown sugar, and salt, stirring well with a whisk. Cut in butter with a pastry blender or 2 knives until mixture resembles coarse meal. Press mixture firmly into a 13 x 9–inch glass or ceramic baking dish coated with cooking spray.
2. Combine figs, 1 cup water, and ¼ cup granulated sugar in a medium saucepan; bring to a boil over medium-high heat. Cook 5 minutes or until figs are tender and sugar dissolves. Cool slightly. Place fig mixture and juice in a blender; process until smooth. Gently spread fig mixture over prepared crust.
3. Place remaining ¼ cup granulated sugar, cheese, vanilla, and egg in a medium bowl; beat with a mixer at medium speed until smooth. Pour over fig mixture; spread to edges. Bake at 350° for 30 minutes or until set and lightly browned around the edges. Cool in pan on a wire rack; sprinkle evenly with powdered sugar. **Serves 30 (serving size: 1 bar).**

CALORIES 125; FAT 3.9g (sat 2.1g, mono 1.4g, poly 0.2g); PROTEIN 1.8g; CARB 21.7g; FIBER 1.5g; CHOL 17mg; IRON 0.7mg; SODIUM 84mg; CALC 33mg

■ BAKING 101 TIP

For easy storing, transfer these bars to an airtight container for up to five days. Or you can store them in the pan they were baked in; just make sure you seal the pan tightly with plastic wrap to keep them fresh.

Toffee Blond Brownies

1 cup packed brown sugar
¼ cup butter, melted
¼ cup egg substitute
2 teaspoons vanilla extract
4.5 ounces all-purpose flour (about 1 cup)
½ teaspoon baking powder
⅛ teaspoon salt
Cooking spray
¼ cup toffee baking bits

1. Preheat oven to 350°. Combine first 4 ingredients in a large bowl, stirring with a whisk. Weigh or lightly spoon flour into a dry measuring cup; level with a knife. Combine flour, baking powder, and salt. Add flour mixture to sugar mixture; stir just until moist.

2. Spread batter into an 8-inch square metal baking pan coated with cooking spray. Sprinkle with toffee bits. Bake at 350° for 22 minutes or until a wooden pick inserted in center comes out almost clean. Cool in pan on a wire rack.

Serves 12 (serving size: 1 brownie).

CALORIES 168; FAT 5.4g (sat 3.2g, mono 1.1g, poly 0.2g); PROTEIN 1.6g; CARB 28.4g; FIBER 0.3g; CHOL 14mg; IRON 1mg; SODIUM 120mg; CALC 31mg

■ BAKING 101 TIP

The toffee bits melt slightly during baking but retain their shape, giving the thin, gooey brownies a crunchy topping.

Peanut Butter–Chocolate Chip Brownies

Cooking spray
4.5 ounces all-purpose flour (about 1 cup)
¼ cup semisweet chocolate minichips
¼ teaspoon baking soda
⅛ teaspoon salt
¾ cup granulated sugar

¼ cup packed dark brown sugar
¼ cup creamy peanut butter
1 tablespoon canola oil
1 teaspoon vanilla extract
1 large egg
1 large egg white

1. Preheat oven to 350°. Coat bottom of an 8-inch square metal baking pan with cooking spray (do not coat sides of pan).
2. Weigh or lightly spoon flour into a dry measuring cup; level with a knife. Combine flour and next 3 ingredients in a bowl. Combine sugars and next 5 ingredients in a bowl; stir until well blended. Add flour mixture, stirring just until blended.
3. Spread batter in prepared pan. Bake at 350° for 25 minutes or until a wooden pick inserted in center comes out almost clean. Cool in pan on a wire rack. **Serves 16 (serving size: 1 brownie).**

CALORIES 125; FAT 4.2g (sat 1.1g, mono 1.9g, poly 1g); PROTEIN 2.7g; CARB 19.8g; FIBER 0.5g; CHOL 14mg; IRON 0.6mg; SODIUM 66mg; CALC 7mg

■ BAKING 101 TIP

Substitute crunchy peanut butter for the creamy variety for added texture in these brownies.

BARS & SQUARES

BARS & SQUARES

Fudgy Brownies

1 cup sugar
2 large eggs
1 tablespoon hot water
2 teaspoons instant coffee granules
¼ cup butter, melted
1 teaspoon vanilla extract

4.5 ounces all-purpose flour (about 1 cup)
⅔ cup unsweetened cocoa
¼ teaspoon salt
Cooking spray
1 tablespoon powdered sugar (optional)

1. Preheat oven to 325°. Place sugar and eggs in a large bowl; beat with a mixer at high speed until thick and pale (about 5 minutes). Combine 1 tablespoon hot water and coffee granules, stirring until coffee granules dissolve. Add coffee mixture, butter, and vanilla to sugar mixture; beat at low speed until combined.

2. Weigh or lightly spoon flour into a dry measuring cup; level with a knife. Combine flour, cocoa, and salt, stirring with a whisk. Gradually add flour mixture to sugar mixture, stirring just until moist (batter will be thick).

3. Spread batter into an 8-inch square metal baking pan coated with cooking spray. Bake at 325° for 23 minutes or until brownies spring back when touched lightly in center. Cool in pan on a wire rack. Sprinkle brownies with powdered sugar, if desired. **Serves 16 (serving size: 1 brownie).**

CALORIES 121; FAT 4.1g (sat 2.3g, mono 1.3g, poly 0.2g); PROTEIN 2.4g; CARB 20.6g; FIBER 1.4g; CHOL 34mg; IRON 1mg; SODIUM 75mg; CALC 10mg

■ BAKING 101 TIP

Beating the sugar and eggs together
incorporates air into the mixture, which acts
as the only leavening in these brownies.
It's important to go the full 5 minutes. This
procedure also creates the crackly surface
on top of the brownies.

Mocha-Toffee Brownies

¼ cup hot water
2 tablespoons instant coffee granules
¼ cup butter
¼ cup semisweet chocolate chips
6.75 ounces all-purpose flour (about 1½ cups)
1⅓ cups sugar
½ cup unsweetened cocoa

1 teaspoon baking powder
½ teaspoon salt
1 teaspoon vanilla extract
2 large eggs
Cooking spray
¼ cup toffee chips

1. Preheat oven to 350°. Combine ¼ cup hot water and coffee granules, stirring until coffee granules dissolve.
2. Combine butter and semisweet chocolate chips in a small microwave-safe bowl. Microwave at HIGH 1 minute or until butter melts; stir until chocolate is smooth.
3. Weigh or lightly spoon flour into dry measuring cups; level with a knife. Combine flour and next 4 ingredients in a large bowl, stirring with a whisk. Combine coffee mixture, butter mixture, vanilla, and eggs in a medium bowl, stirring with a whisk. Add coffee mixture to flour mixture; stir just until combined.
4. Spread batter evenly into a 9-inch square metal baking pan coated with cooking spray. Sprinkle evenly with toffee chips. Bake at 350° for 25 minutes or until a wooden pick inserted in center comes out with moist crumbs. Cool in pan on a wire rack. **Serves 20 (serving size: 1 brownie).**

CALORIES 145; FAT 4.8g (sat 2.4g, mono 1.8g, poly 0.3g); PROTEIN 2.2g; CARB 24.9g; FIBER 1.1g; CHOL 30mg; IRON 0.9mg; SODIUM 121mg; CALC 23mg

■ BAKING 101 TIP
Coffee and toffee give these rich chocolate brownies a unique twist. If you have any leftovers, store them in an airtight container for up to a week or wrap tightly in foil and freeze for up to four months.

Cream Cheese–Swirled Brownies

6.75 ounces all-purpose flour (about 1½ cups)	¾ cup 2% reduced-fat milk
2 cups sugar, divided	¾ teaspoon vanilla extract, divided
½ cup unsweetened cocoa	2 large eggs
½ teaspoon baking powder	Cooking spray
¼ teaspoon salt	½ cup (4 ounces) ⅓-less-fat cream cheese, softened
¼ cup butter	1 large egg white
2 ounces unsweetened chocolate, chopped	

1. Preheat oven to 350°. Weigh or lightly spoon flour into dry measuring cups; level with a knife. Combine flour, 1¾ cups sugar, cocoa, baking powder, and salt in a large bowl, stirring well with a whisk.

2. Place butter and chocolate in a microwave-safe bowl; microwave at HIGH 45 seconds or until melted, stirring once. Combine milk, ½ teaspoon vanilla, and eggs, stirring well with a whisk. Add chocolate mixture and milk mixture to flour mixture; beat with a mixer at medium speed until blended. Spoon batter evenly into a 13 x 9–inch metal baking pan coated with cooking spray.

3. Place remaining ¼ cup sugar, remaining ¼ teaspoon vanilla, cheese, and egg white in a medium bowl; beat at medium speed until well blended using clean, dry beaters. Drizzle cheese mixture evenly over chocolate mixture; swirl batters together using the tip of a knife. Bake at 350° for 30 minutes or until batter begins to pull away from sides of pan. Cool completely in pan on a wire rack. **Serves 28 (serving size: 1 brownie).**

CALORIES 131; FAT 4.3g (sat 2.6g, mono 1.3g, poly 0.2g); PROTEIN 2.5g; CARB 21.5g; FIBER 0.8g; CHOL 23mg; IRON 1.3mg; SODIUM 69mg; CALC 23mg

■ BAKING 101 TIP

For moist and fudgy results, be careful not to overbake. When the brownies are perfectly done, the edges of the batter will just begin to pull away from the pan.

prep
time:
15
minutes

prep
time:
10
minutes

Swag Bars

1¾ cups creamy peanut butter
¾ cup sugar
¾ cup light-colored corn syrup
3½ cups (4 ounces) whole-grain flaked cereal, finely crushed

1½ cups (6 ounces) chopped lightly salted, dry-roasted peanuts
Cooking spray
2 ounces dark chocolate, chopped

1. Combine first 3 ingredients in a heavy saucepan over medium-high heat. Cook 4 minutes or just until mixture begins to boil, stirring constantly. Remove from heat; stir in cereal and peanuts. Spread mixture evenly into a 13 x 9–inch metal baking pan coated with cooking spray. Let stand until set.
2. Place dark chocolate in a small microwave-safe bowl. Microwave at HIGH 1 minute or until chocolate melts, stirring every 20 seconds. Drizzle chocolate evenly over peanut mixture. Cut into 36 bars while warm. **Serves 36** (serving size: 1 bar).

CALORIES 155; FAT 9.2g (sat 1.9g, mono 4.2g, poly 2.5g); PROTEIN 4.5g; CARB 16.2g; FIBER 1.5g; CHOL 0mg; IRON 2.3mg; SODIUM 121mg; CALC 113mg

■ BAKING 101 TIP

These no-bake bars come together quickly with common pantry ingredients. Make sure the cereal is well crushed (try packing it in a sealed zip-top plastic bag and using a rolling pin) so it incorporates into the peanut butter mixture.

Peanut Butter–Crispy Rice Bars

⅓ **cup creamy peanut butter**
1 **tablespoon butter**
1 **(10½-ounce) bag miniature marshmallows**

6 **cups oven-toasted rice cereal**
Cooking spray
¾ **cup peanut butter chips**

1. Place peanut butter and butter in a large microwave-safe bowl. Microwave at HIGH 45 seconds or until mixture melts. Add marshmallows; microwave at HIGH 1½ minutes or until smooth, stirring every 30 seconds. Add cereal to peanut butter mixture; toss until well combined. Lightly coat hands with cooking spray; press cereal mixture evenly into a 13 x 9–inch metal baking pan coated with cooking spray. Let stand until set.
2. Place peanut butter chips in a small microwave-safe bowl. Microwave at HIGH 30 seconds or until chips melt. Spoon melted chips into a small heavy-duty zip-top plastic bag; seal. Snip a tiny hole in 1 corner of bag; drizzle melted chips over cereal mixture. Cool slightly. **Serves 24 (serving size: 1 bar).**

CALORIES 118; FAT 3.9g (sat 1.3g, mono 1.5g, poly 0.8g); PROTEIN 2.6g; CARB 19g; FIBER 0.7g; CHOL 1mg; IRON 0.4mg; SODIUM 93mg; CALC 9mg

■ BAKING 101 TIP

This mixture is very sticky. Coating your hands with cooking spray before pressing it into the pan makes the process easier.

Green Pumpkinseed and Cranberry Crispy Bars

Cooking spray
- ½ cup raw green pumpkinseed kernels
- ¼ cup butter
- 5 cups miniature marshmallows
- 1 teaspoon vanilla extract
- ⅛ teaspoon salt
- 5 cups oven-toasted rice cereal
- 1 cup dried cranberries

1. Heat a large skillet over medium-high heat. Coat pan with cooking spray. Add pumpkinseeds; cook 4 minutes or until seeds begin to pop and lightly brown, stirring frequently. Remove from heat; cool.

2. Melt butter in a large saucepan over medium heat. Stir in marshmallows; cook 2 minutes or until smooth, stirring constantly. Remove from heat; stir in vanilla and salt. Stir in pumpkinseeds, cereal, and cranberries.

3. Scrape mixture into a 13 x 9–inch glass or ceramic baking dish coated with cooking spray. Lightly coat hands with cooking spray; press cereal mixture evenly into pan. Cool completely. **Serves 16 (serving size: 1 bar).**

CALORIES 152; FAT 4.9g (sat 2.2g, mono 1.4g, poly 1g); PROTEIN 1.9g; CARB 26.3g; FIBER 0.7g; CHOL 8mg; IRON 0.9mg; SODIUM 115mg; CALC 4.7mg

■ **BAKING 101 TIP**

Green pumpkinseeds are also sometimes sold as pepitas. In humid weather, cool the bars in the refrigerator to prevent them from becoming too sticky.

prep
time:
10
minutes

Cupcakes
& Cakes

Banana Cupcakes with Peanut Butter Frosting

Cupcakes:

- ¼ cup butter, softened
- 1 cup granulated sugar
- 4 large egg whites
- ½ cup mashed ripe banana (about 1 large)
- 1 teaspoon vanilla extract
- 7.75 ounces all-purpose flour (about 1¾ cups)
- 1 teaspoon baking powder
- ¼ teaspoon salt
- ½ cup 1% low-fat milk
- Cooking spray

Frosting:

- ¼ cup (2 ounces) ⅓-less-fat cream cheese, softened
- ¼ cup creamy peanut butter
- 3 tablespoons butter, softened
- 1½ cups powdered sugar
- ½ teaspoon vanilla extract
- Dash of salt
- Unsalted, dry-roasted peanuts, chopped (optional)
- Banana slices (optional)

1. Preheat oven to 350°. To prepare cupcakes, place ¼ cup butter and granulated sugar in a large bowl; beat with a mixer at medium speed until blended. Add egg whites; beat well. Add mashed banana and 1 teaspoon vanilla; beat 1 minute.

2. Weigh or lightly spoon flour into dry measuring cups; level with a knife. Combine flour, baking powder, and ¼ teaspoon salt in a bowl, stirring with a whisk. Add flour mixture and milk alternately to sugar mixture, beginning and ending with flour mixture.

3. Place 12 paper muffin cup liners in muffin cups; coat liners with cooking spray. Spoon batter into prepared muffin cups. Bake at 350° for 20 minutes or until a wooden pick inserted in center comes out clean. Cool 5 minutes in pan on a wire rack. Remove from pan; cool completely on wire rack.

4. To prepare frosting, combine cream cheese, peanut butter, and 3 tablespoons butter in a medium bowl; beat until light and fluffy. Add powdered sugar, ½ teaspoon vanilla, and dash of salt. Spread frosting evenly over cupcakes. Garnish with chopped peanuts and banana slices, if desired. **Serves 12 (serving size: 1 cupcake).**

CALORIES 319; FAT 11.4g (sat 5.6g, mono 3.4g, poly 1.3g); PROTEIN 5.6g; CARB 50g; FIBER 1.2g; CHOL 21mg; IRON 1.2mg; SODIUM 219mg; CALC 51mg

prep
time:
15
minutes

■ **BAKING 101 TIP**
Garnish these cupcakes—reminiscent of peanut
butter and banana sandwiches—with the banana
just before serving.

Lemon-Scented Blueberry Cupcakes

Cupcakes:

- 6.75 ounces all-purpose flour (about 1½ cups)
- 2 tablespoons all-purpose flour, divided
- 10 tablespoons granulated sugar
- 1½ teaspoons baking powder
- ¼ teaspoon salt
- ⅛ teaspoon baking soda
- ¼ cup butter, melted
- 1 large egg
- ½ cup low-fat buttermilk
- ½ cup 2% reduced-fat milk
- 1 teaspoon grated lemon rind
- ¾ cup fresh or frozen blueberries, thawed
- Cooking spray

Frosting:

- ¼ cup (2 ounces) ⅓-less-fat cream cheese, softened
- 2 tablespoons butter, softened
- 1 teaspoon grated lemon rind
- 1 teaspoon vanilla extract
- ⅛ teaspoon salt
- 1½ cups sifted powdered sugar
- 2 teaspoons fresh lemon juice
- Fresh blueberries (optional)
- Grated lemon rind (optional)

1. Preheat oven to 350°. To prepare cupcakes, weigh or lightly spoon 6.75 ounces flour (about 1½ cups) into dry measuring cups; level with a knife. Combine 6.75 ounces and 1 tablespoon flour, granulated sugar, baking powder, ¼ teaspoon salt, and baking soda in a large bowl, stirring with a whisk. Combine melted butter and egg in another large bowl, stirring with a whisk. Add buttermilk, milk, and 1 teaspoon rind to butter mixture; stir with a whisk. Add buttermilk mixture to flour mixture, stirring just until moist. Toss blueberries with remaining 1 tablespoon flour. Fold blueberries into batter.

2. Place 12 paper muffin cup liners in muffin cups; coat liners with cooking spray. Spoon batter into prepared muffin cups. Bake at 350° for 25 minutes or until a wooden pick inserted in center comes out clean. Cool 5 minutes in pan on a wire rack. Remove from pan; cool completely on wire rack.

3. To prepare frosting, place cream cheese and next 4 ingredients in a bowl; beat with a mixer at medium speed just until blended. Gradually add powdered sugar (do not overbeat). Stir in juice. Spread frosting evenly over cupcakes; garnish with blueberries and grated lemon rind, if desired. Store, covered, in refrigerator. **Serves 12 (serving size: 1 cupcake).**

CALORIES 236; FAT 7.7g (sat 4.6g, mono 2g, poly 0.4g); PROTEIN 3.7g; CARB 38.7g; FIBER 0.7g; CHOL 38mg; IRON 1mg; SODIUM 230mg; CALC 71mg

■ BAKING 101 TIP

Tossing fresh blueberries with a little bit of flour is an
important step. It prevents the blueberries from sinking
to the bottom of the cupcakes while they bake.

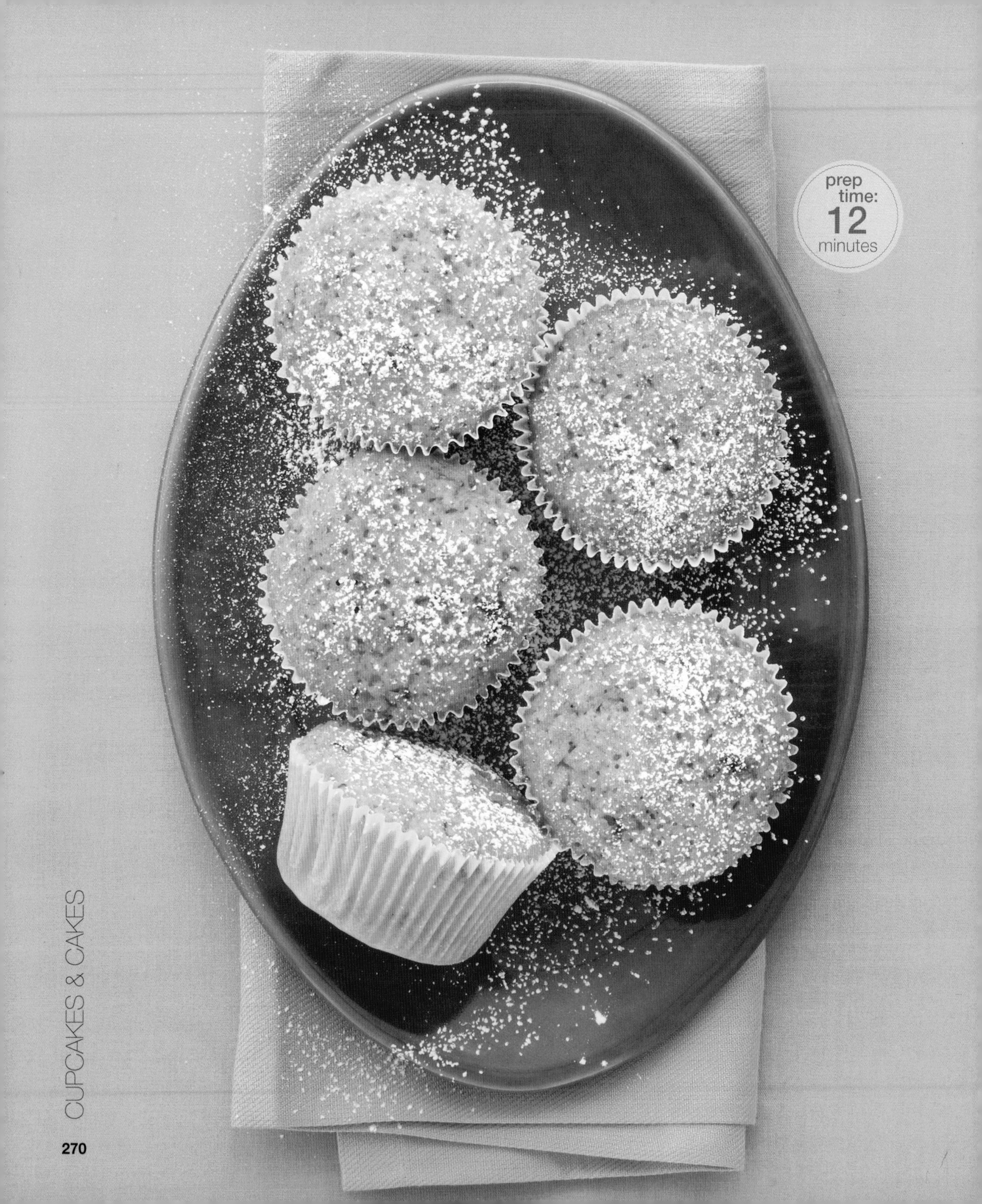

prep time: 12 minutes

Carrot-Chocolate Cupcakes

1 pound carrots, peeled and sliced
1¾ cups granulated sugar
6 tablespoons canola oil
⅓ cup low-fat buttermilk
3 large eggs
9 ounces all-purpose flour (about 2 cups)

2 teaspoons baking soda
½ teaspoon salt
1 ounce semisweet chocolate, finely chopped
Cooking spray
3 tablespoons powdered sugar

1. Preheat oven to 350°. Place carrots in a food processor; process until finely minced. Combine carrots, granulated sugar, oil, buttermilk, and eggs in a large bowl. Weigh or lightly spoon flour into dry measuring cups; level with a knife. Combine flour, baking soda, and salt, stirring with a whisk. Add flour mixture to carrot mixture; stir until smooth. Stir in chocolate.

2. Place 22 muffin cup liners in muffin cups; coat liners with cooking spray. Spoon batter into prepared muffin cups. Bake at 350° for 22 minutes or until a wooden pick inserted in center comes out clean. Cool 10 minutes in pans on wire racks. Remove from pan; cool completely on wire racks. Sift powdered sugar over cupcakes. **Serves 22 (serving size: 1 cupcake).**

CALORIES 156; FAT 3.6g (sat 0.9g, mono 2.3g, poly 0.2g); PROTEIN 2.5g; CARB 28.8g; FIBER 1g; CHOL 29mg; IRON 0.7mg; SODIUM 226mg; CALC 15mg

◼ BAKING 101 TIP

Because there is no frosting on these cupcakes, they freeze well: Store them (without the powdered sugar) in a heavy-duty zip-top plastic bag. To thaw, wrap each cupcake in a paper towel, and microwave at MEDIUM for 15 to 25 seconds. Or if you have more time, let them sit at room temperature until thawed, and then dust with powdered sugar.

Coconut Cupcakes with Lime Buttercream Frosting

Cupcakes:

- 4.5 ounces all-purpose flour (about 1 cup)
- 3 tablespoons potato starch
- 1 teaspoon baking powder
- ½ teaspoon salt
- ¾ cup granulated sugar
- 2 tablespoons butter, softened
- 1 large egg
- 1 large egg white
- ⅔ cup fat-free milk
- 2 tablespoons flaked sweetened coconut
- ½ teaspoon vanilla extract
- Cooking spray

Frosting:

- 3 tablespoons butter, softened
- ½ teaspoon grated lime rind
- 1 tablespoon fresh lime juice
- 1 teaspoon half-and-half
- 1⅓ cups sifted powdered sugar
- Grated lime rind (optional)

1. Preheat oven to 350°. To prepare cupcakes, weigh or lightly spoon flour into a dry measuring cup; level with a knife. Combine flour and next 3 ingredients in a small bowl, stirring with a whisk. Combine ¾ cup granulated sugar and 2 tablespoons butter in a large bowl; beat with a mixer at medium speed until blended (mixture will be the consistency of damp sand). Add egg and egg white, 1 at a time, beating well after each addition. Add flour mixture and milk alternately to egg mixture, beginning and ending with flour mixture. Fold in coconut and vanilla.

2. Place 12 paper muffin cup liners in muffin cups; coat liners with cooking spray. Spoon batter into prepared muffin cups. Bake at 350° for 18 minutes or until a wooden pick inserted in center comes out clean. Cool 2 minutes in pan on a wire rack. Remove from pan; cool completely on wire rack.

3. To prepare frosting, combine 3 tablespoons butter and next 3 ingredients in a medium bowl; beat with a mixer at medium speed until smooth. Gradually add powdered sugar, beating just until smooth. Spread about 2½ teaspoons frosting onto each cupcake. Garnish with lime rind, if desired. **Serves 12 (serving size: 1 cupcake).**

CALORIES 196; FAT 5.6g (sat 3.4g, mono 1.4g, poly 0.3g); PROTEIN 2.5g; CARB 34.8g; FIBER 0.3g; CHOL 31mg; IRON 0.7mg; SODIUM 179mg; CALC 52mg

■ BAKING 101 TIP

You'll find potato starch on the baking aisle at most local supermarkets and health-food stores. It helps ensure that the cupcakes will have a fine crumb and moist texture.

prep
time:
15
minutes

prep
time:
18
minutes

BAKING 101 TIP

Sifting the flour and powdered sugar mixture
thoroughly three times incorporates the
powdered sugar for a light, tender cupcake.
If you don't have a sifter, use a whisk to
thoroughly combine the ingredients.

Lemon Angel Food Cupcakes

Cupcakes:

- 2 ounces cake flour (about ½ cup)
- ¾ cup powdered sugar
- 5 large egg whites
- ⅛ teaspoon salt
- ¾ teaspoon cream of tartar
- ½ cup granulated sugar
- 2 teaspoons grated lemon rind
- ½ teaspoon vanilla extract
- Cooking spray

Frosting:

- ¼ cup butter, softened
- 2 cups powdered sugar
- 1 tablespoon 1% low-fat milk
- 1 to 2 tablespoons fresh lemon juice
- Fresh strawberry halves (optional)

1. Preheat oven to 350°. To prepare cupcakes, weigh or lightly spoon flour into a dry measuring cup; level with a knife. Sift together flour and ¾ cup powdered sugar into a medium bowl; repeat procedure 2 times.

2. Beat egg whites and salt with a mixer at high speed until frothy (about 1 minute). Add cream of tartar, and beat until soft peaks form. Add ½ cup granulated sugar, 1 tablespoon at a time, beating until stiff peaks form. Sprinkle flour mixture over egg white mixture, ¼ cup at a time; fold in after each addition. Stir in rind and vanilla.

3. Place 16 paper muffin cup liners in muffin cups; coat liners with cooking spray. Spoon batter into prepared muffin cups. Bake at 350° for 18 minutes or until lightly browned. Remove from pans; cool completely on wire racks.

4. To prepare frosting, beat butter with a mixer at high speed until fluffy. Gradually add 2 cups powdered sugar; beat at low speed just until blended. Add milk and 1 tablespoon lemon juice; beat until fluffy. Add more lemon juice as needed to adjust the consistency. Spread 2 tablespoons lemon frosting over each cupcake. Garnish with strawberry halves, if desired. **Serves 16 (serving size: 1 cupcake).**

CALORIES 144; FAT 2.9g (sat 1.8g, mono 0.8g, poly 0.1g); PROTEIN 1.6g; CARB 28.9g; FIBER 0.1g; CHOL 8mg; IRON 0.3mg; SODIUM 58mg; CALC 4mg

Coffee Cupcakes

Cupcakes:
- 2 tablespoons boiling water
- 4 teaspoons instant espresso granules or 8 teaspoons instant coffee granules
- ⅓ cup low-fat buttermilk
- 5.6 ounces all-purpose flour (about 1¼ cups)
- ½ teaspoon baking soda
- ¼ teaspoon salt
- ¾ cup granulated sugar
- 5 tablespoons butter, softened
- 2 teaspoons vanilla extract
- 2 large eggs
- Cooking spray

Syrup:
- ¼ cup granulated sugar
- ¼ cup water
- 2 tablespoons instant espresso granules or ¼ cup instant coffee granules
- 2 tablespoons light-colored corn syrup
- ¼ teaspoon vanilla extract
- 2 tablespoons powdered sugar

1. Preheat oven to 350°. To prepare cupcakes, combine 2 tablespoons boiling water and 4 teaspoons espresso granules, stirring until granules dissolve. Stir in buttermilk.

2. Weigh or lightly spoon flour into dry measuring cups; level with a knife. Combine flour, baking soda, and salt, stirring well with a whisk. Place ¾ cup granulated sugar, butter, and 2 teaspoons vanilla in a large bowl; beat with a mixer at medium speed until well blended (about 3 minutes). Add eggs, 1 at a time, beating well after each addition. Add flour mixture and buttermilk mixture alternately to sugar mixture, beginning and ending with flour mixture.

3. Place 12 paper muffin cup liners in muffin cups; coat liners with cooking spray. Spoon batter into prepared muffin cups. Bake at 350° for 20 minutes or until a wooden pick inserted in center comes out clean. Cool 10 minutes in pan on a wire rack. Remove from pan; cool on a wire rack.

4. To prepare syrup, combine ¼ cup granulated sugar, ¼ cup water, 2 tablespoons espresso granules, corn syrup, and ¼ teaspoon vanilla in a small saucepan; bring to a boil. Reduce heat; simmer 3 minutes. Pierce cupcake tops several times with a wooden skewer. Brush espresso syrup evenly over cupcakes. Cool completely on wire rack. Sift powdered sugar over cupcakes. **Serves 12 (serving size: 1 cupcake).**

CALORIES 192; FAT 5.8g (sat 3.3g, mono 1.8g, poly 0.4g); PROTEIN 3g; CARB 31.8g; FIBER 0.4g; CHOL 49mg; IRON 0.9mg; SODIUM 173mg; CALC 19mg

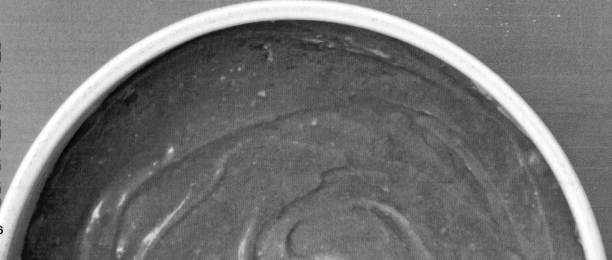

■ BAKING 101 TIP

If you prefer a single-layer cake to cupcakes, use
a 9-inch square metal baking pan or round cake
pan. Bake the cake at 350° for 25 minutes or until a
wooden pick inserted in the center comes out clean.

prep time:
15
minutes

Double-Ginger Cupcakes with Lemon Glaze

Cupcakes:
- 4.5 ounces all-purpose flour (about 1 cup)
- 1 teaspoon ground ginger
- ½ teaspoon baking powder
- ½ teaspoon baking soda
- ½ teaspoon ground cinnamon
- ¼ teaspoon salt
- ⅛ teaspoon ground allspice
- ½ cup low-fat buttermilk
- ¼ cup molasses
- ½ cup packed brown sugar
- 3 tablespoons butter, softened
- 1½ teaspoons grated peeled fresh ginger
- 1 large egg, lightly beaten

Glaze:
- ⅔ cup sifted powdered sugar
- 3 to 4 teaspoons fresh lemon juice
- Grated lemon rind (optional)

1. Preheat oven to 350°. To prepare cupcakes, weigh or lightly spoon flour into a dry measuring cup; level with a knife. Combine flour and next 6 ingredients, stirring with a whisk. Combine buttermilk and molasses, stirring with a whisk. Place brown sugar and butter in a large bowl; beat with a mixer at medium speed until well blended (about 1 minute). Add fresh ginger and egg; beat well. Beating at low speed, add flour mixture and buttermilk mixture alternately to butter mixture, beginning and ending with flour mixture. Beat just until blended.

2. Place 12 foil muffin cup liners in muffin cups. Spoon batter into prepared muffin cups. Bake at 350° for 20 minutes or until a wooden pick inserted in center comes out clean. Cool 10 minutes in pan on a wire rack. Remove from pan; cool on wire rack.

3. To prepare glaze, combine powdered sugar and juice, stirring until smooth. Drizzle over warm cupcakes. Garnish with lemon rind, if desired. **Serves 12 (serving size: 1 cupcake).**

CALORIES 155; FAT 3.5g (sat 2g, mono 0.9g, poly 0.2g); PROTEIN 2g; CARB 29.6g; FIBER 0.4g; CHOL 26mg; IRON 1.2mg; SODIUM 145mg; CALC 51mg

■ **BAKING 101 TIP**
Foil liners give the batter something to cling to as the cupcakes bake, which helps them rise better.

prep time: **17** minutes

Red Velvet Cupcakes

Cupcakes:

- 10 ounces cake flour (about 2½ cups)
- 3 tablespoons unsweetened cocoa
- 1 teaspoon baking soda
- 1 teaspoon baking powder
- 1 teaspoon kosher salt
- 1½ cups granulated sugar
- 6 tablespoons butter, softened
- 2 large eggs
- 1¼ cups nonfat buttermilk
- 2 tablespoons red food coloring (about 1 ounce)
- 1½ teaspoons white vinegar
- 1½ teaspoons vanilla extract
- Cooking spray

Frosting:

- 5 tablespoons butter, softened
- 4 teaspoons nonfat buttermilk
- 1 (8-ounce) block cream cheese, softened
- 3½ cups powdered sugar
- 1¼ teaspoons vanilla extract

1. Preheat oven to 350°. To prepare cupcakes, weigh or lightly spoon flour into dry measuring cups; level with a knife. Combine flour and next 4 ingredients in a medium bowl, stirring with a whisk. Place granulated sugar and butter in a large bowl; beat with a mixer at medium speed until well blended (about 3 minutes). Add eggs, 1 at a time, beating well after each addition. Add flour mixture and 1¼ cups buttermilk alternately to sugar mixture, beginning and ending with flour mixture. Add food coloring, white vinegar, and 1½ teaspoons vanilla; beat well.
2. Place 24 paper muffin cup liners in muffin cups; coat liners with cooking spray. Spoon batter into prepared muffin cups. Bake at 350° for 20 minutes or until a wooden pick inserted in center comes out clean. Cool 10 minutes in pans on wire racks. Remove from pan; cool completely on wire racks.
3. To prepare frosting, beat 5 tablespoons butter, 4 teaspoons nonfat buttermilk, and cream cheese with a mixer at high speed until fluffy. Gradually add powdered sugar; beat until smooth. Add 1¼ teaspoons vanilla; beat well. Spread frosting evenly over cupcakes. **Serves 24 (serving size: 1 cupcake).**

CALORIES 202; FAT 7.3g (sat 4.3g, mono 1.9g, poly 0.4g); PROTEIN 2.2g; CARB 32.8g; FIBER 0.3g; CHOL 32mg; IRON 0.9mg; SODIUM 196mg; CALC 37mg

■ BAKING 101 TIP

Cake flour is a fine-textured soft wheat flour that makes cakes and cupcakes more tender. Look for it with the cake mixes in the supermarket; make sure you buy plain cake flour, not self-rising.

Chocolate Cupcakes with Vanilla Cream Cheese Frosting

Cupcakes:
- 1 cup granulated sugar
- ¼ cup canola oil
- ½ teaspoon vanilla extract
- 4 large egg whites
- 6.75 ounces all-purpose flour (about 1½ cups)
- ½ cup unsweetened cocoa
- 1 teaspoon baking soda
- 1 teaspoon instant coffee granules
- ½ teaspoon baking powder
- ¼ teaspoon salt
- 1 cup nonfat buttermilk
- Cooking spray

Frosting:
- 1 cup powdered sugar
- ½ teaspoon vanilla extract
- 1 (8-ounce) block ⅓-less-fat cream cheese, softened
- Dash of salt

1. Preheat oven to 350°. To prepare cupcakes, place first 4 ingredients in a large bowl; beat with a mixer at medium speed until well blended (about 2 minutes).

2. Weigh or lightly spoon flour into dry measuring cups; level with a knife. Combine flour and next 5 ingredients, stirring well with a whisk. Add flour mixture and buttermilk alternately to sugar mixture, beginning and ending with flour mixture; mix after each addition just until blended.

3. Place 16 paper muffin cup liners in muffin cups; coat liners with cooking spray. Spoon about 2½ tablespoons batter into each cup. Bake at 350° for 18 minutes or until a wooden pick inserted in center comes out with moist crumbs clinging (do not overbake). Remove cupcakes from pans; cool on wire racks.

4. To prepare frosting, combine powdered sugar and remaining ingredients in a medium bowl. Beat with a mixer at medium speed until combined. Increase speed to medium-high, and beat until smooth. Spread about 1 tablespoon frosting on top of each cupcake. **Serves 16 (serving size: 1 cupcake).**

CALORIES 203; FAT 6.8g (sat 2.1g, mono 3g, poly 1.3g); PROTEIN 4.8g; CARB 32.4g; FIBER 1.2g; CHOL 8mg; IRON 1.3mg; SODIUM 211mg; CALC 53mg

prep
time:
15
minutes

■ BAKING 101 TIP

For a thicker frosting, cover and chill for 10 minutes
before spreading it on the cupcakes. Refrigerate the
frosted cupcakes overnight; cover lightly with plastic
wrap, or store them in an airtight container.

prep
time:
11
minutes

Double-Chocolate Cupcakes

4.5	ounces all-purpose flour (about 1 cup)	4	large egg whites
⅓	cup unsweetened cocoa	½	cup low-fat buttermilk
1	teaspoon baking soda	1¼	ounces dark (70 percent cocoa) chocolate, finely chopped
⅛	teaspoon salt		Cooking spray
⅔	cup granulated sugar	2	tablespoons powdered sugar
¼	cup butter, softened		
1	teaspoon vanilla extract		

1. Preheat oven to 350°. Weigh or lightly spoon flour into a dry measuring cup; level with a knife. Combine flour and next 3 ingredients, stirring with a whisk. Place granulated sugar and butter in a large bowl; beat with a mixer at medium speed until well combined (about 3 minutes). Add vanilla and egg whites, beating well. Add flour mixture and buttermilk alternately to granulated sugar mixture, beginning and ending with flour mixture. Fold in chocolate.
2. Place 12 paper muffin cup liners in muffin cups; coat liners with cooking spray. Spoon batter into prepared muffin cups. Bake at 350° for 18 minutes or until cupcakes spring back when touched lightly in center or until a wooden pick inserted in center comes out clean. Remove from pan; cool completely on a wire rack. Sift powdered sugar over cupcakes just before serving. **Serves 12 (serving size: 1 cupcake).**

CALORIES 150; FAT 5.2g (sat 3.2g, mono 1.2g, poly 0.2g); PROTEIN 3.1g; CARB 24g; FIBER 1.1g; CHOL 11mg; IRON 1mg; SODIUM 125mg; CALC 42mg

■ BAKING 101 TIP

These cupcakes are so easy to make. And since they're studded with dark chocolate chunks, simply dust with powdered sugar to finish them.

Autumn Apple Cake

6.75 ounces all-purpose flour (about 1½ cups)
2 teaspoons baking powder
¼ teaspoon salt
¼ teaspoon ground cinnamon
¾ cup granulated sugar
5 tablespoons butter, softened
1 teaspoon vanilla extract
1 large egg

½ cup 2% reduced-fat milk
1 cup finely chopped peeled Pink Lady apple
    (about 1 medium)
½ cup golden raisins
¼ cup finely chopped walnuts, toasted
Cooking spray
1 tablespoon all-purpose flour
1 teaspoon powdered sugar

1. Preheat oven to 350°. Weigh or lightly spoon 6.75 ounces flour (about 1½ cups) into dry measuring cups; level with a knife. Combine 6.75 ounces flour and next 3 ingredients in a small bowl, stirring with a whisk. Place granulated sugar and butter in a large bowl; beat with a mixer until well blended. Beat in vanilla and egg. Add flour mixture and milk alternately to butter mixture, beginning and ending with flour mixture. Fold in apple, raisins, and walnuts.
2. Coat a 9-inch round cake pan with cooking spray, and dust with 1 tablespoon flour. Scrape batter into prepared pan. Bake at 350° for 30 minutes or until a wooden pick inserted in center comes out clean. Cool 10 minutes in pan on a wire rack. Remove from pan; cool completely on wire rack. Sift powdered sugar over top of cake. **Serves 8 (serving size: 1 wedge).**

CALORIES 304; FAT 10.6g (sat 5.1g, mono 2.5q, poly 2.2g); PROTEIN 4.8g; CARB 48.9g; FIBER 1.7g; CHOL 42mg; IRON 1.7mg; SODIUM 263mg; CALC 106mg

■ **BAKING 101 TIP**

Use a sweet, crisp apple—such as Pink Lady, Braeburn, or Sundowner—in this recipe.

prep
time:
16
minutes

Carrot Cake

Cake:
- 6.75 ounces all-purpose flour (about 1½ cups)
- 1⅓ cups granulated sugar
- ½ cup flaked sweetened coconut
- ⅓ cup chopped pecans, toasted
- 2 teaspoons baking soda
- 2 teaspoons ground cinnamon
- 1 teaspoon salt
- 3 tablespoons canola oil
- 2 large eggs
- 2 cups grated carrot
- 1½ cups canned crushed pineapple, drained
- Cooking spray

Frosting:
- 2 tablespoons butter, softened
- 1 (8-ounce) block ⅓-less-fat cream cheese, softened
- 3 cups powdered sugar
- 2 teaspoons vanilla extract
- Additional grated carrot (optional)

1. Preheat oven to 350°. To prepare cake, weigh or lightly spoon flour into dry measuring cups; level with a knife. Combine flour and next 6 ingredients in a large bowl, stirring well with a whisk. Combine oil and eggs. Stir egg mixture, grated carrot, and pineapple into flour mixture. Spoon batter into a 13 x 9–inch metal baking pan coated with cooking spray. Bake at 350° for 35 minutes or until a wooden pick inserted in center comes out clean. Cool completely in pan on a wire rack.

2. To prepare frosting, combine butter and cream cheese in a large bowl. Beat with a mixer at medium speed until smooth. Beat in powdered sugar and vanilla just until smooth. Spread frosting evenly over cake. Garnish each serving with grated carrot, if desired. **Serves 16 (serving size: 1 piece).**

CALORIES 322; FAT 10.4g (sat 4.2g, mono 3.2g, poly 1.5g); PROTEIN 4.1g; CARB 54.4g; FIBER 1.4g; CHOL 40mg; IRON 1mg; SODIUM 403mg; CALC 29mg

■ BAKING 101 TIP

Softened butter should be pliable but not easily spreadable. To test it, put your finger in the butter; you should be able to see your fingerprint without it being too soft. If you're in a hurry, don't put the butter in the microwave; it's easy to get it too soft. For a quick-softening method, cut the butter into 1-tablespoon pieces and leave it at room temperature for 10 to 15 minutes.

prep time: 19 minutes

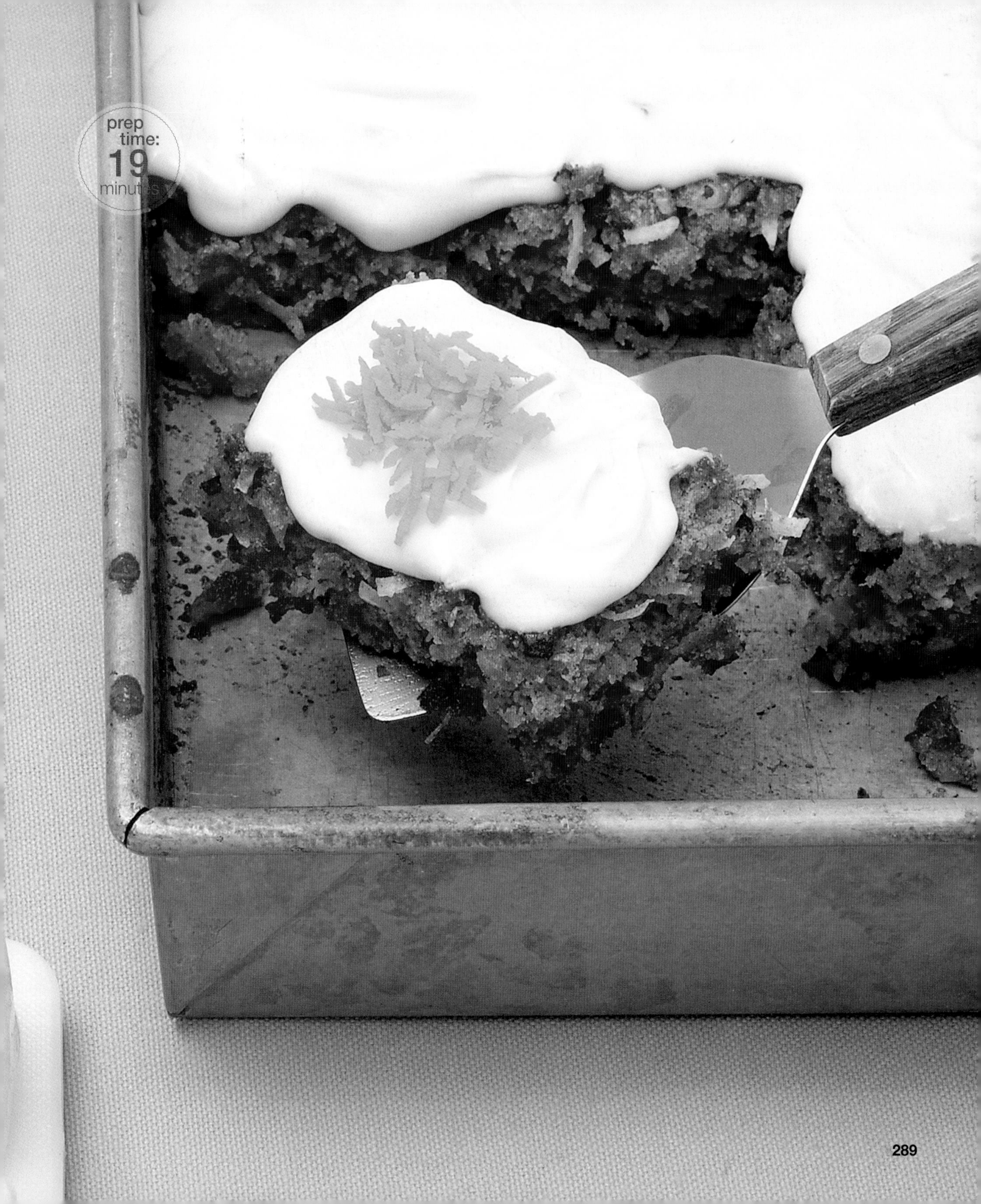

Cardamom-Date Snack Cake

Cake:

Cooking spray

9 ounces all-purpose flour (about 2 cups)
1 teaspoon baking powder
1 teaspoon baking soda
½ teaspoon salt
½ teaspoon ground cardamom
½ teaspoon ground cinnamon
5 tablespoons butter, softened
1 cup packed brown sugar

1 cup applesauce
1 teaspoon vanilla extract
3 large eggs
¾ cup chopped pitted dates

Topping:

⅓ cup sliced almonds
3 tablespoons all-purpose flour
3 tablespoons brown sugar
2 tablespoons butter, melted

1. Preheat oven to 350°. To prepare cake, coat a 9-inch square metal baking pan with cooking spray; set aside.

2. Weigh or lightly spoon 9 ounces flour (about 2 cups) into dry measuring cups; level with a knife. Combine flour and next 5 ingredients in a large bowl; make a well in center of mixture. Combine 5 tablespoons butter and next 4 ingredients in a medium bowl; beat with a mixer at medium speed until blended. Add to flour mixture; stir just until moist. Stir in dates. Spoon batter into prepared pan.

3. To prepare topping, combine almonds and remaining ingredients, stirring with a fork until blended. Sprinkle evenly over batter. Bake at 350° for 35 minutes or until a wooden pick inserted in center comes out clean. Cool completely in pan on a wire rack. **Serves 16 (serving size: 1 piece).**

CALORIES 230; FAT 7.6g (sat 3.6g, mono 2.6g, poly 0.8g); PROTEIN 3.9g; CARB 37.8g; FIBER 1.7g; CHOL 53mg; IRON 1.6mg; SODIUM 248mg; CALC 52mg

■ BAKING 101 TIP

The dates make this treat extremely moist and tender;
use a serrated knife to make a cleaner cut.

prep
time:
13
minutes

Frosted Pumpkin Cake

Cake:
- 10.1 ounces all-purpose flour (about 2¼ cups)
- 2½ teaspoons baking powder
- 2 teaspoons ground cinnamon
- ¼ teaspoon salt
- 1 cup packed brown sugar
- ¼ cup butter, softened
- 1 teaspoon vanilla extract
- 2 large eggs
- 1 (15-ounce) can pumpkin puree
- Cooking spray

Frosting:
- 2 tablespoons butter, softened
- ½ teaspoon vanilla extract
- 1 (8-ounce) block ⅓-less-fat cream cheese
- 2 cups sifted powdered sugar

1. Preheat oven to 350°. To prepare cake, weigh or lightly spoon flour into dry measuring cups; level with a knife. Combine flour and next 3 ingredients in a small bowl, stirring with a whisk. Combine brown sugar, ¼ cup butter, and 1 teaspoon vanilla in a large bowl; beat with a mixer at medium speed until well blended. Add eggs, 1 at a time, beating well after each addition. Add pumpkin; mix well. Fold in flour mixture.

2. Spoon batter into a 13 x 9–inch metal baking pan coated with cooking spray. Bake at 350° for 25 minutes or until a wooden pick inserted in center comes out clean. Cool completely in pan on a wire rack.

3. To prepare frosting, combine 2 tablespoons butter, ½ teaspoon vanilla, and cream cheese in a medium bowl; beat with a mixer at medium speed until combined. Gradually add powdered sugar, beating until well combined. Spread frosting evenly over top of cake. **Serves 24 (serving size: 1 piece).**

CALORIES 178; FAT 5.5g (sat 3.3g, mono 1.3g, poly 0.3g); PROTEIN 3g; CARB 30g; FIBER 0.9g; CHOL 32mg; IRON 1.2mg; SODIUM 135mg; CALC 62mg

■ BAKING 101 TIP

We call for a metal baking pan for this cake; if you use a glass or ceramic baking dish, which conducts heat better than metal, reduce the oven temperature to 325°, and begin checking for doneness after 20 minutes.

Ginger Cake

½ cup granulated sugar
½ cup applesauce
2 tablespoons canola oil
2 large eggs
1 cup molasses
6.75 ounces all-purpose flour (about 1½ cups)
½ cup flaxseed meal
½ cup toasted wheat germ
2 teaspoons baking soda

½ to 1 teaspoon ground cinnamon
½ to 1 teaspoon ground cloves
½ to 1 teaspoon ground ginger
¼ teaspoon salt
1 cup hot water
Cooking spray
Powdered sugar (optional)
Fresh apple slices (optional)

1. Preheat oven to 350°. Combine first 3 ingredients in a large bowl; beat with a mixer at medium speed until well blended (about 1 minute). Add eggs, 1 at a time, beating well after each addition. Stir in molasses.
2. Weigh or lightly spoon flour into dry measuring cups; level with a knife. Combine flour and next 7 ingredients in a large bowl. Add flour mixture and 1 cup hot water alternately to sugar mixture, beginning and ending with flour mixture.
3. Spoon batter into a 13 x 9–inch metal baking pan coated with cooking spray. Bake at 350° for 30 minutes or until a wooden pick inserted in center comes out clean. Cool in pan on a wire rack. Garnish with powdered sugar and apple slices, if desired. **Serves 12 (serving size: 1 piece).**

CALORIES 253; FAT 6.1g (sat 0.7g, mono 2.2g, poly 2.7g); PROTEIN 4.8g; CARB 46.1g; FIBER 2.6g; CHOL 35mg; IRON 2.9mg; SODIUM 284mg; CALC 81mg

■ **BAKING 101 TIP**

Adding flaxseed meal and wheat germ increases
the fiber, protein, and calcium in each serving.
Powdered sugar and thinly cut apple slices
make a pretty garnish.

prep
time:
12
minutes

Fudgy Sheet Cake

Cake:
- ½ cup unsweetened cocoa
- ½ cup boiling water
- 7.5 ounces sifted cake flour (about 2 cups)
- 1 teaspoon baking soda
- ½ teaspoon salt
- 1½ cups granulated sugar
- ⅓ cup butter, softened
- 2 teaspoons vanilla extract
- 2 large eggs
- 1 cup low-fat buttermilk
- Cooking spray

Frosting:
- 1½ cups sifted powdered sugar
- 3 tablespoons unsweetened cocoa
- 2 tablespoons 1% low-fat milk
- 1 teaspoon butter, softened
- ½ teaspoon vanilla extract

1. Preheat oven to 350°. To prepare cake, combine ½ cup cocoa and ½ cup boiling water in a small bowl, stirring with a whisk until smooth; cool. Combine flour, baking soda, and salt, stirring well with a whisk. Place granulated sugar, butter, and 2 teaspoons vanilla in a large bowl; beat with a mixer at medium speed until well blended. Add eggs, 1 at a time, beating well after each addition. Beat in cocoa mixture. Add flour mixture and buttermilk alternately to sugar mixture, beginning and ending with flour mixture and beating well after each addition.

2. Spoon batter into a 13 x 9–inch metal baking pan coated with cooking spray. Bake at 350° for 30 minutes or until cake springs back when lightly touched. Cool 10 minutes in pan on a wire rack.

3. To prepare frosting, combine powdered sugar and 3 tablespoons cocoa in a medium bowl, stirring well with a whisk. Add milk, 1 teaspoon butter, and ½ teaspoon vanilla; stir with a whisk until smooth. Spread frosting evenly over cake. **Serves 16 (serving size: 1 piece).**

CALORIES 242; FAT 5.6g (sat 3.2g, mono 1.5g, poly 0.3g); PROTEIN 3.5g; CARB 46.6g; FIBER 1.5g; CHOL 38mg; IRON 1.9mg; SODIUM 209mg; CALC 33mg

■ BAKING 101 TIP

Frosting a cake soon after it cools helps maintain its moistness. If you must delay that step, wrap the cake in plastic wrap once it's completely cooled.

Sticky Date and Coconut Cake

Cake:
- 1 cup chopped pitted dates
- 1 cup water
- 3 tablespoons butter
- 1 teaspoon baking soda
- Dash of salt
- 6.75 ounces all-purpose flour (about 1½ cups)
- 1 teaspoon baking powder
- ½ teaspoon salt
- 1 cup granulated sugar
- 1 teaspoon vanilla extract
- 1 large egg, lightly beaten
- Cooking spray

Topping:
- ⅔ cup packed brown sugar
- ½ cup flaked sweetened coconut
- 2½ tablespoons butter
- 2 teaspoons fat-free milk

1. Preheat oven to 350°. To prepare cake, combine first 5 ingredients in a small saucepan; bring to a boil, stirring occasionally. Remove from heat, and let stand 10 minutes or until dates are tender.

2. Weigh or lightly spoon flour into dry measuring cups; level with a knife. Combine flour, baking powder, and ½ teaspoon salt in a bowl. Stir in date mixture, granulated sugar, vanilla, and egg until well combined. Pour batter into a 9-inch springform pan coated with cooking spray. Bake at 350° for 20 minutes.

3. To prepare topping, combine brown sugar and remaining ingredients in a small saucepan; bring to a boil. Reduce heat, and simmer 1 minute. Pour brown sugar mixture over cake; bake an additional 13 minutes or until a wooden pick inserted in center comes out clean. Cool 5 minutes in pan on a wire rack. Run a knife around outside edge. Cool completely on wire rack. **Serves 12 (serving size: 1 wedge).**

CALORIES 268; FAT 6.5g (sat 4.2g, mono 1.6g, poly 0.3g); PROTEIN 2.5g; CARB 51.6g; FIBER 1.7g; CHOL 31mg; IRON 1.2mg; SODIUM 313mg; CALC 46mg

■ BAKING 101 TIP

A springform pan is a round, deep pan with tall, removable sides. Be sure to coat the bottom and sides of the pan with cooking spray so this puddinglike cake doesn't stick.

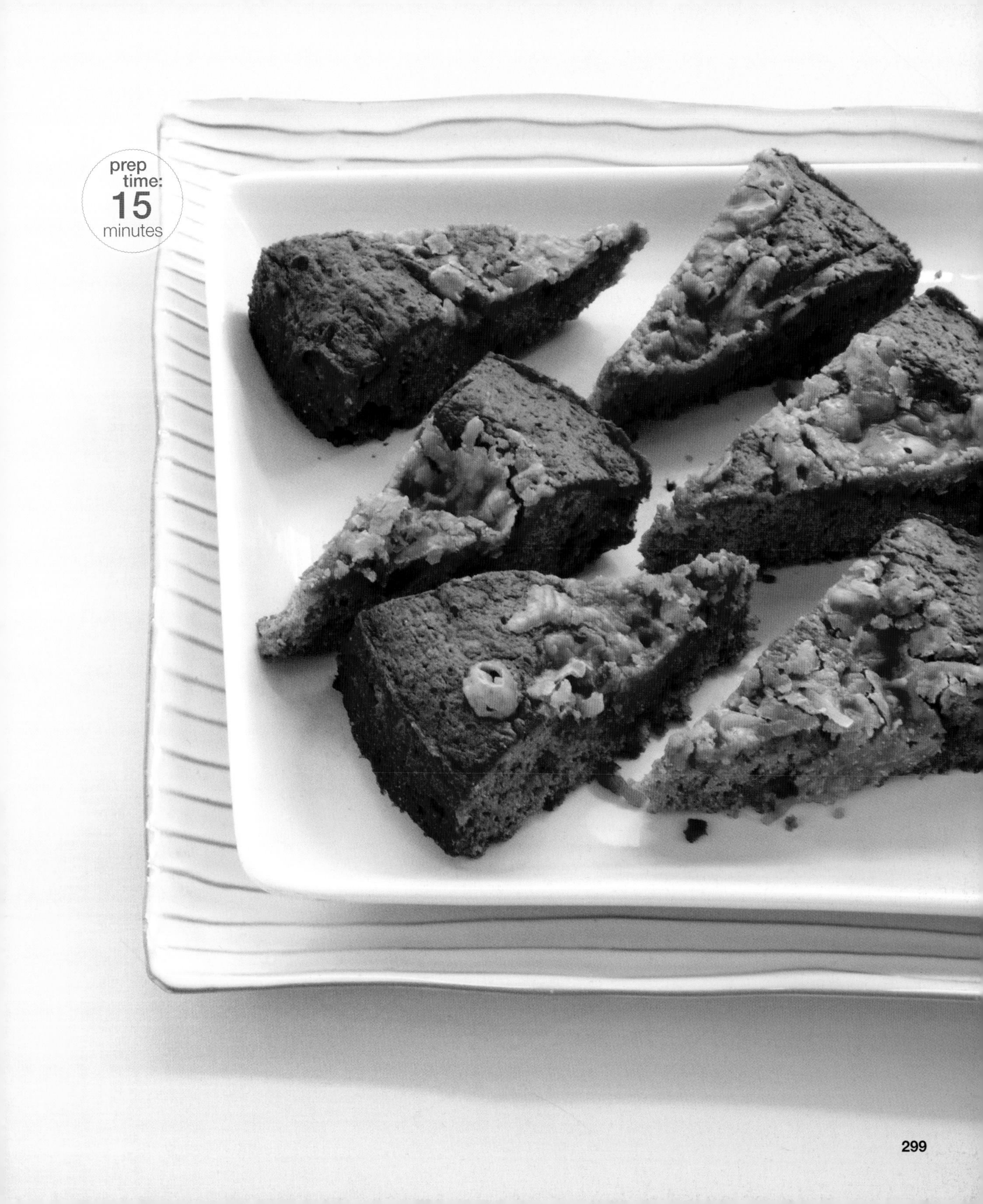

prep time: 15 minutes

Vanilla-Buttermilk Pound Cakes

13.5 ounces all-purpose flour (about 3 cups)
  1 teaspoon baking powder
  ½ teaspoon baking soda
  ½ teaspoon salt
  2 cups sugar
  ¾ cup butter, softened
  1 teaspoon vanilla extract
  3 large eggs
  1⅓ cups low-fat buttermilk
Cooking spray

1. Preheat oven to 350°. Weigh or lightly spoon flour into dry measuring cups; level with a knife. Combine flour and next 3 ingredients, stirring with a whisk. Place sugar, butter, and vanilla in a large bowl; beat with a mixer at medium speed until light and fluffy. Add eggs, 1 at a time, beating well after each addition. Add flour mixture and buttermilk alternately to sugar mixture, beginning and ending with flour mixture.

2. Spoon batter into 5 (5¾ x 3¾–inch) loaf pans coated with cooking spray. Bake at 350° for 40 minutes or until a wooden pick inserted in center comes out clean. Cool 10 minutes in pans on wire racks. Remove from pans. Cool completely on wire racks. **Serves 30 (serving size: 1 slice).**

CALORIES 144; FAT 5.1g (sat 3.1g, mono 1.4g, poly 0.2g); PROTEIN 2.2g; CARB 22.3g; FIBER 0.3g; CHOL 34mg; IRON 0.7mg; SODIUM 95mg; CALC 25mg

■ BAKING 101 TIP

You can also prepare these cakes in two (8 x 4–inch) loaf pans, if you'd like. Bake at 350° for one hour or until done. To freeze extra pound cakes, let the cakes cool completely on a wire rack; then cut into individual slices and place them in a heavy-duty zip-top plastic bag. Remove excess air from the bag, then seal and place it in your freezer for up to four months. To thaw, let the slices stand at room temperature.

prep
time:
12
minutes

Double-Banana Pound Cake

Cooking spray
3 tablespoons dry breadcrumbs
13.5 ounces all-purpose flour (about 3 cups)
1 teaspoon baking powder
¼ teaspoon salt
¼ teaspoon ground mace
1 cup mashed ripe banana (about 2 large)

½ cup fat-free milk
½ cup banana liqueur
¾ cup butter, softened
2 cups granulated sugar
1½ teaspoons vanilla extract
3 large eggs
1 tablespoon powdered sugar

1. Preheat oven to 350°. Coat a 10-inch tube pan with cooking spray; dust with breadcrumbs.

2. Weigh or lightly spoon flour into dry measuring cups; level with a knife. Combine flour and next 3 ingredients in a bowl, stirring well with a whisk. Combine mashed banana, milk, and banana liqueur in a bowl. Place butter in a large bowl; beat with a mixer at medium speed until light and fluffy. Gradually add granulated sugar and vanilla, and beat until well blended. Add eggs, 1 at a time, beating well after each addition. Add flour mixture and banana mixture alternately to sugar mixture, beating at low speed, beginning and ending with flour mixture.

3. Spoon batter into prepared pan. Bake at 350° for 1 hour or until a wooden pick inserted in center comes out clean. Cool 10 minutes in pan on a wire rack. Remove from pan; cool completely on wire rack. Sift powdered sugar over top of cake. **Serves 18 (serving size: 1 slice).**

CALORIES 286; FAT 8.9g (sat 5.1g, mono 2.6g, poly 0.5g); PROTEIN 3.8g; CARB 44.8g; FIBER 0.9g; CHOL 58mg; IRON 1.3mg; SODIUM 163mg; CALC 37mg

■ BAKING 101 TIP

This cake packs a double punch of banana with the fruit and liqueur. You can omit the liqueur if you like. (The banana flavor will be less pronounced.) Just increase the milk to one cup total. You can use a 12-cup Bundt pan instead of the 10-inch tube pan; just reduce the oven temperature to 325°.

Glazed Lemon-Buttermilk Cake

Cake:
- 3 tablespoons grated lemon rind (about 2 lemons)
- 3 tablespoons fresh lemon juice (about 1 lemon)
- 13.5 ounces all-purpose flour (about 3 cups)
- 1 teaspoon baking powder
- ¾ teaspoon salt
- ½ teaspoon baking soda
- ½ cup butter, softened
- 1½ cups plus 2 tablespoons granulated sugar, divided
- 3 large eggs
- 1 cup low-fat buttermilk
- Cooking spray

Glaze:
- 1 cup powdered sugar
- 1½ tablespoons fresh lemon juice
- 1 tablespoon low-fat buttermilk
- 1 teaspoon grated lemon rind (optional)

1. Preheat oven to 350°. To prepare cake, combine rind and 3 tablespoons juice in a small bowl. Set aside.

2. Weigh or lightly spoon flour into dry measuring cups; level with a knife. Combine flour and next 3 ingredients in a large bowl, stirring well with a whisk.

3. Place butter in a large bowl; beat with a mixer at medium speed until light and fluffy. Gradually add 1½ cups granulated sugar and rind mixture, beating until well blended. Add eggs, 1 at a time, beating well after each addition. Add flour mixture and 1 cup buttermilk alternately to sugar mixture, beating at low speed, beginning and ending with flour mixture.

4. Coat a 12-cup Bundt pan with cooking spray; dust with remaining 2 tablespoons granulated sugar. Spoon batter into prepared pan. Bake at 350° for 45 minutes or until a wooden pick inserted in center comes out clean. Cool 10 minutes in pan on a wire rack. Remove from pan; cool on wire rack.

5. To prepare glaze, combine powdered sugar, 1½ tablespoons juice, and 1 tablespoon buttermilk in a small bowl, stirring until smooth. Drizzle glaze over warm cake. Garnish with grated lemon rind once glaze is set, if desired.

Serves 16 (serving size: 1 slice).

CALORIES 267; FAT 7g (sat 4g, mono 1.9g, poly 0.4g); PROTEIN 4.3g; CARB 47.3g; FIBER 0.8g; CHOL 56mg; IRON 1.3mg; SODIUM 252mg; CALC 46mg

■ BAKING 101 TIP
Fresh lemon juice and grated rind lend lots of lemon flavor to this cake.

Pies, Cobblers & Crumbles

Mini Apple Pies

2½ cups thinly sliced peeled Braeburn apple (about 1 pound)

2½ cups thinly sliced peeled Cortland apple (about 1 pound)

1.1 ounces all-purpose flour (about ¼ cup)

1 cup sugar

¼ teaspoon ground cinnamon

⅛ teaspoon ground allspice

1½ (14.1-ounce) packages refrigerated pie dough

Cooking spray

1 tablespoon chilled butter, cut into small pieces

1 teaspoon vanilla extract

1 tablespoon whole milk

1. Preheat oven to 350°. Place apple in a large bowl. Weigh or lightly spoon flour into a dry measuring cup; level with a knife. Combine flour and next 3 ingredients in a small bowl. Sprinkle sugar mixture over apple; toss well to coat.

2. Working with 1 dough portion at a time, roll dough into a 12-inch circle on a lightly floured surface. Cut piecrust into 12 (5½-inch) circles, rerolling dough as needed. Fit 6 dough circles into 6 (4½-inch) dishes or tart pans coated with cooking spray, allowing dough to extend over edges. Spoon apple mixture evenly into prepared dishes, and dot evenly with 1 tablespoon butter. Drizzle apple mixture evenly with vanilla. Top with remaining 6 dough circles; press edges of dough together. Fold edges under, and flute. Brush surface of dough with milk. Cut 3 (1-inch) slits in top of dough to allow steam to escape. Bake at 350° for 45 minutes or until apples are tender. **Serves 12 (serving size: ½ mini pie).**

CALORIES 328; FAT 14g (sat 5.3g, mono 3.9g, poly 3.3g); PROTEIN 1.4g; CARB 48.7g; FIBER 0.7g; CHOL 8mg; IRON 0.2mg; SODIUM 211mg; CALC 5mg

■ BAKING 101 TIP

You'll need to reroll the pie dough twice to get all the dough circles you need to make these mini pies. You can substitute Rome or Gala apples in this recipe, if you'd like.

Fresh Cherry Pie

- 2 tablespoons uncooked quick-cooking tapioca
- 6 cups pitted sweet cherries
- ¾ cup granulated sugar
- ¼ cup cornstarch
- 1 tablespoon fresh lemon juice
- ¼ teaspoon almond extract
- ⅛ teaspoon salt
- 1 (14.1-ounce) package refrigerated pie dough
- Cooking spray
- 2 tablespoons water
- 1 large egg white
- 2 tablespoons turbinado sugar

1. Place tapioca in a spice or coffee grinder; process until finely ground. Combine tapioca and next 6 ingredients in a large bowl; toss well. Let cherry mixture stand 30 minutes; stir to combine.

2. Preheat oven to 400°. Roll 1 (9-inch) dough portion into an 11-inch circle on a lightly floured surface. Fit dough into a 9-inch pie plate coated with cooking spray, allowing dough to extend over edge of plate. Spoon cherry mixture and any remaining liquid into crust. Roll remaining 9-inch dough portion into a 12-inch circle on a lightly floured surface. Cut dough into 12 (1-inch-wide) strips; arrange in a lattice pattern over cherry mixture. Fold edges under, and crimp.

3. Combine 2 tablespoons water and egg white in a small bowl. Brush egg white mixture over dough on top of pie, and sprinkle dough evenly with 2 tablespoons turbinado sugar. Bake at 400° for 20 minutes. Shield edges of piecrust with foil, and bake an additional 40 minutes or until crust is golden brown and filling is thick and bubbly. Cool 45 minutes in pan on a wire rack. **Serves 12 (serving size: 1 wedge).**

CALORIES 282; FAT 9.9g (sat 4.1g, mono 4.3g, poly 1.2g); PROTEIN 2.5g; CARB 47.3g; FIBER 1.7g; CHOL 7mg; IRON 0.3mg; SODIUM 161mg; CALC 11mg

■ BAKING 101 TIP

Some pie connoisseurs prefer sour cherries; we love the way sweet ones work in this filling. They create a not-too-sweet cherry pie that is delicious on its own and even better served warm with a scoop of vanilla ice cream.

prep
time:
25
minutes

Pear-Cranberry Pie with Oatmeal Streusel

Streusel:
- ¾ cup old-fashioned rolled oats
- ½ cup packed brown sugar
- ½ teaspoon ground cinnamon
- ¼ teaspoon ground nutmeg
- Dash of salt
- 2 tablespoons chilled butter, cut into small pieces

Filling:
- 3 cups (½-inch) cubed peeled Anjou pear (2 large)
- 2 cups fresh cranberries
- ⅔ cup packed brown sugar
- 2½ tablespoons cornstarch

Remaining ingredient:
- 1 unbaked 9-inch deep-dish pastry shell

1. Preheat oven to 350°. To prepare streusel, combine first 5 ingredients in a medium bowl; cut in butter with a pastry blender or 2 knives until mixture resembles coarse meal.

2. To prepare filling, combine pear and next 3 ingredients in a large bowl; toss well to combine. Spoon pear mixture into pastry shell; sprinkle streusel over pear mixture. Bake at 350° for 1 hour or until bubbly and streusel is browned. Cool at least 1 hour on a wire rack. **Serves 12 (serving size: 1 wedge).**

CALORIES 240; FAT 8.2g (sat 2.4g, mono 3.1g, poly 0.8g); PROTEIN 1.6g; CARB 41.5g; FIBER 2.4g; CHOL 5mg; IRON 0.8mg; SODIUM 118mg; CALC 27mg

■ SHORTCUT TIP

A made-from-scratch piecrust is delicious, but we used a prepared pastry shell to save time; it still creates a stellar dessert. If you can't find fresh cranberries, use thawed frozen ones.

313

Lemon Pie

5 medium lemons
2 cups granulated sugar
½ (14.1-ounce) package refrigerated pie dough
Cooking spray
3 tablespoons all-purpose flour
¼ teaspoon salt
4 large eggs, lightly beaten
½ cup heavy whipping cream
2 tablespoons powdered sugar
Fresh raspberries (optional)

1. Grate ½ cup rind from lemons. Remove white pithy part of rind; discard. Chop lemons; discard seeds. Combine rind, chopped lemon, and granulated sugar in a large bowl; toss well. Cover and let stand at room temperature 24 hours, stirring occasionally.

2. Preheat oven to 450°. Roll dough into an 11-inch circle on a lightly floured surface; fit dough into a 9-inch pie plate coated with cooking spray. Fold edges under, and flute. Add flour, salt, and eggs to lemon mixture, stirring with a whisk until combined. Pour lemon mixture into crust. Bake at 450° for 15 minutes.

3. Reduce oven temperature to 375°. Shield edges of piecrust with foil; bake at 375° for 25 minutes or until filling is set. Cool completely on a wire rack.

4. Combine cream and powdered sugar. Beat with a mixer at high speed until stiff peaks form. Serve with pie. Top with raspberries, if desired. **Serves 12 (serving size: 1 wedge and 1½ tablespoons whipped cream).**

CALORIES 277; FAT 9.8g (sat 4.7g, mono 3.2g, poly 0.9g); PROTEIN 3.2g; CARB 46.9g; FIBER 1.3g; CHOL 86mg; IRON 0.4mg; SODIUM 162mg; CALC 30mg

■ BAKING 101 TIP

To flute the edges of the pie, use two fingers on one hand and one finger on the other to pinch the dough.

Cinnamon Streusel–Topped Pumpkin Pie

Filling:
- ¾ teaspoon ground cinnamon
- ¼ teaspoon ground allspice
- ¼ teaspoon ground ginger
- ¼ teaspoon ground nutmeg
- ⅛ teaspoon ground cloves
- 2 large eggs
- 1 (15-ounce) can unsweetened pumpkin
- 1 (14-ounce) can fat-free sweetened condensed milk

Streusel:
- 1.5 ounces all-purpose flour (about ⅓ cup)
- ⅓ cup packed dark brown sugar
- ¼ cup old-fashioned rolled oats
- ¼ cup chopped pecans
- ¾ teaspoon ground cinnamon
- ⅛ teaspoon ground ginger
- 2 tablespoons chilled butter, cut into small pieces
- 2 teaspoons water

Crust:
- ½ (14.1-ounce) package refrigerated pie dough
- Cooking spray

1. Preheat oven to 375°. To prepare filling, combine first 8 ingredients in a large bowl, stirring with a whisk.

2. To prepare crust, roll dough into an 11-inch circle on a lightly floured surface. Fit dough into a 9-inch pie plate coated with cooking spray. Fold edges under; flute.

3. To prepare streusel, weigh or lightly spoon flour into a dry measuring cup; level with a knife. Combine flour and next 5 ingredients in a bowl. Cut in butter with a pastry blender or 2 knives until crumbly. Sprinkle with 2 teaspoons water, tossing with a fork just until lightly moist.

4. Pour pumpkin mixture into crust; sprinkle with streusel. Place pie on a baking sheet. Bake at 375° for 50 minutes or until a knife inserted in center comes out clean. Remove from baking sheet; cool completely on a wire rack.

Serves 12 (serving size: 1 wedge).

CALORIES 262; FAT 9g (sat 3.6g, mono 3.3g, poly 1.2g); PROTEIN 5.5g; CARB 41.1g; FIBER 1.7g; CHOL 46mg; IRON 1mg; SODIUM 136mg; CALC 110mg

■ BAKING 101 TIP

Using fat-free sweetened condensed milk in place of regular maintains sweetness and richness with fewer calories.

prep
time:
12
minutes

Five-Spice Sweet Potato Pie

2 pounds sweet potatoes (about 5 medium)
¾ cup packed brown sugar
½ cup 2% reduced-fat milk
2 tablespoons butter, softened
1 teaspoon vanilla extract
½ teaspoon ground cinnamon
½ teaspoon five-spice powder or pumpkin pie spice
¼ teaspoon salt
¼ teaspoon ground nutmeg
3 large eggs, lightly beaten
½ (14.1-ounce) package refrigerated pie dough
Cooking spray
Frozen fat-free whipped topping, thawed (optional)

1. Preheat oven to 375°. Pierce sweet potatoes several times with a fork. Place sweet potatoes on a paper towel in microwave. Microwave at HIGH 12 minutes or until tender, rearranging potatoes after 6 minutes. Let stand 5 minutes. Peel and discard skins. Place pulp in a medium bowl, and mash. Add brown sugar and next 8 ingredients to pulp. Beat with a mixer at medium speed until well blended.
2. Roll dough into an 11-inch circle on a lightly floured surface. Fit dough into a 9-inch pie plate coated with cooking spray. Fold edges under, and flute. Pour sweet potato mixture into crust. Bake at 375° for 55 minutes or until a knife inserted in center comes out clean. Cool pie completely on a wire rack. Serve with whipped topping, if desired.
Serves 10 (serving size: 1 wedge).

CALORIES 289; FAT 9.7g (sat 4.2g, mono 3.7g, poly 0.4g); PROTEIN 4.9g; CARB 46.1g; FIBER 3.1g; CHOL 74mg; IRON 1.3mg; SODIUM 220mg; CALC 74mg

■ BAKING 101 TIP

Five-spice powder is a blend of cinnamon, cloves, fennel seed, star anise, and Szechuan peppercorns. You can find it in the spice aisle of most supermarkets. If five-spice powder is unavailable, use pumpkin pie spice.

Oatmeal-Pecan Pie

½ (14.1-ounce) package refrigerated pie dough
Cooking spray
1 cup packed dark brown sugar
1 cup light corn syrup
⅔ cup old-fashioned rolled oats
½ cup chopped pecans

2 tablespoons butter, melted
1 teaspoon vanilla extract
¼ teaspoon salt
2 large eggs, lightly beaten
2 large egg whites, lightly beaten

1. Preheat oven to 325°. Roll dough into an 11-inch circle on a lightly floured surface. Fit dough into a 9-inch pie plate coated with cooking spray. Fold edges under, and flute.

2. Combine brown sugar and remaining ingredients, stirring well with a whisk. Pour into prepared crust. Bake at 325° for 50 minutes or until center is set. Cool completely on a wire rack. **Serves 12 (serving size: 1 wedge).**

CALORIES 311; FAT 11.3g (sat 3.5g, mono 5g, poly 2.6g); PROTEIN 3.2g; CARB 51.4g; FIBER 1g; CHOL 42mg; IRON 0.8mg; SODIUM 181mg; CALC 30mg

■ **BAKING 101 TIP**

Rolled oats add heartiness and whole grains to the filling of this classic dessert. Plus, our lightened version will save you about 200 calories per slice when compared to a traditional pecan pie.

PIES, COBBLERS & CRUMBLES

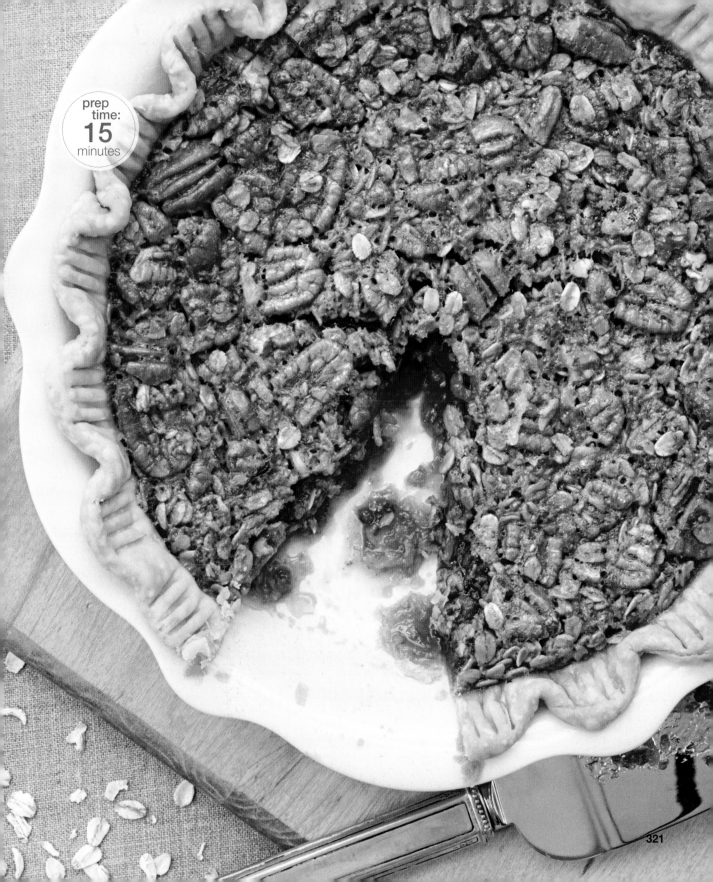

Peanut Butter Pie

1 cup powdered sugar

1 cup natural-style creamy peanut butter

1 (8-ounce) block ⅓-less-fat cream cheese, softened

1 (14-ounce) can fat-free sweetened condensed milk

12 ounces frozen fat-free whipped topping, thawed

2 (6-ounce) reduced-fat graham cracker crusts

20 teaspoons fat-free chocolate sundae syrup

1. Combine first 3 ingredients in a large bowl; beat with a mixer at medium speed until smooth. Add milk; beat until combined. Fold in whipped topping. Divide mixture evenly between crusts; chill 8 hours or until set (pies will have a soft, fluffy texture). Cut into wedges; drizzle evenly with chocolate syrup. **Serves 20 (serving size: 1 wedge and 1 teaspoon syrup).**

CALORIES 302; FAT 11.7g (sat 3.4g, mono 4.5g, poly 3.1g); PROTEIN 6.5g; CARB 42.7g; FIBER 0.9g; CHOL 11mg; IRON 0.5mg; SODIUM 205mg; CALC 65mg

■ BAKING 101 TIP

Full-fat peanut butters trump reduced-fat flavor, and they supply heart-healthy monounsaturated fats. (Choose butters without trans fats.) Reduced-fat spreads offer little calorie savings, and you're ditching good-for-you fats.

PIES, COBBLERS & CRUMBLES

Easy Caramel-Banana Galette

¼ **cup golden raisins**
2 **tablespoons dark rum**
½ **(14.1-ounce) package refrigerated pie dough**
Cooking spray

3 **cups (¼-inch-thick) diagonally sliced ripe banana (about 1½ pounds)**
½ **cup sugar**
2 **tablespoons water**

1. Combine raisins and rum in a small bowl; let stand at least 30 minutes. Set aside.

2. Preheat oven to 425°. Roll dough into a 10½-inch circle on a lightly floured surface, and place on a foil-lined baking sheet coated with cooking spray. Arrange banana slices in concentric circles on crust, leaving a 1-inch border. Fold a 2-inch dough border over banana slices, pressing gently to seal (dough will partially cover slices). Bake at 425° for 30 minutes.

3. Combine sugar and 2 tablespoons water in a small saucepan; cook over medium heat until golden (about 8 minutes). Remove from heat; carefully stir in raisin mixture until combined. Cool slightly. Pour over banana slices.

Serves 6 (serving size: 1 wedge).

CALORIES 318; FAT 9.7g (sat 2.4g, mono 4g, poly 2.5g); PROTEIN 3.3g; CARB 57.3g; FIBER 2.5g; CHOL 0mg; IRON 0.9mg; SODIUM 160mg; CALC 35mg

■ SHORTCUT TIP

The only trick to making this simple dessert is leaving the caramel unstirred for 8 minutes; stirring can cause it to harden. To simplify the topping, substitute bottled fat-free caramel sauce for the sugar and water. Heat the sauce in the microwave for 1 minute, and then stir in the raisin mixture.

PIES, COBBLERS & CRUMBLES

kitchenessentials
from Calphalon

Nectarine Tarte Tatin

7 medium nectarines, halved and pitted
½ cup sugar
2 tablespoons water
1½ teaspoons fresh lemon juice

2 teaspoons butter
¾ teaspoon vanilla extract
½ (14.1-ounce) package refrigerated pie dough

1. Preheat oven to 425°. Set aside 1 nectarine half. Quarter remaining 13 nectarine halves.

2. Place sugar, 2 tablespoons water, and juice in a 12-inch ovenproof stainless-steel skillet over medium heat; cook until sugar dissolves, stirring gently as needed to dissolve sugar evenly. Continue cooking 2 minutes or until golden (do not stir). Remove from heat; stir in butter and vanilla. Let stand for 3 minutes.

3. Place nectarine half, cut side down, in center of sugar mixture; arrange nectarine quarters, cut sides down, around center. Return pan to medium heat. Cook 5 minutes or until sugar mixture is bubbly (do not stir). Remove from heat; let stand 3 minutes.

4. Roll dough into a 12-inch circle on a lightly floured surface. Place dough over nectarine mixture, fitting dough between nectarines and pan.

5. Bake at 425° for 15 minutes or until lightly browned. Remove from oven, and cool 10 minutes. Carefully invert tart onto a serving plate. **Serves 10 (serving size: 1 wedge).**

CALORIES 183; FAT 6.6g (sat 2.9g, mono 2.7g, poly 0.8g); PROTEIN 1.8g; CARB 30.4g; FIBER 1.6g; CHOL 6mg; IRON 0.3mg; SODIUM 84mg; CALC 6mg

■ **BAKING 101 TIP**

Using an ovenproof stainless-steel skillet to caramelize the sugar is helpful. A pan with a dark surface doesn't allow you to detect the sugar's color changes as easily.

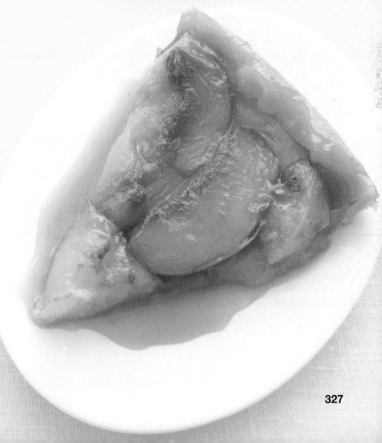

French Apple Tart

½ (14.1-ounce) package refrigerated pie dough
¼ cup sugar
½ teaspoon ground cinnamon
2 pounds Golden Delicious apples, peeled, cored, and thinly sliced

2½ tablespoons honey
½ teaspoon vanilla extract

1. Preheat oven to 425°. Roll dough into a 12-inch circle on a lightly floured surface. Place on a 12-inch pizza pan. Combine sugar and cinnamon. Sprinkle 1 tablespoon sugar mixture over dough. Arrange apple slices spokelike on top of dough, working from outside edge of dough to center. Sprinkle apple slices with remaining sugar mixture. Bake at 425° for 30 minutes or until apples are tender and golden.

2. Combine honey and vanilla in a microwave-safe bowl. Microwave at HIGH 40 seconds. Brush honey mixture over warm tart. Serve warm. **Serves 8 (serving size: 1 wedge).**

CALORIES 220; FAT 7.3g (sat 2.9g, mono 3.2g, poly 0.9g); PROTEIN 0.6g; CARB 39g; FIBER 1.9g; CHOL 5mg; IRON 0.2mg; SODIUM 100mg; CALC 6mg

■ BAKING 101 TIP

This dramatic 12-inch tart uses only six ingredients and bakes in just half an hour. Use a paring knife to prepare the apples for this simple dessert.

Strawberry-Rhubarb Tart

½ **(14.1-ounce) package refrigerated pie dough**
2 **cups sliced rhubarb**
½ **cup sugar**
2 **tablespoons cornstarch**

2 **teaspoons water**
¾ **teaspoon ground cinnamon, divided**
3 **cups sliced strawberries**
1 **tablespoon sugar**

1. Preheat oven to 400°. Roll dough into a 12-inch circle on a lightly floured surface. Press dough into bottom and up sides of a 10-inch removable-bottom tart pan. Line bottom of dough with a piece of foil; arrange pie weights or dried beans on foil. Bake at 400° for 5 minutes. Remove pie weights and foil. Bake an additional 5 minutes. Cool on a wire rack.

2. Combine rhubarb, ½ cup sugar, cornstarch, 2 teaspoons water, and ½ teaspoon cinnamon in a medium saucepan. Bring to a boil; reduce heat, and simmer 5 minutes or until rhubarb is tender, stirring frequently. Remove from heat, and stir in strawberries. Spoon strawberry mixture into prepared crust. Combine remaining ¼ teaspoon cinnamon and 1 tablespoon sugar; sprinkle evenly over tart.

3. Place tart on a baking sheet. Bake at 400° for 30 minutes or until filling is set. Cool on a wire rack. **Serves 8 (serving size: 1 wedge).**

CALORIES 203; FAT 7.2g (sat 3g, mono 1.7g, poly 1.9g); PROTEIN 1.6g; CARB 34g; FIBER 2.1g; CHOL 5mg; IRON 0.4mg; SODIUM 101mg; CALC 36mg

■ BAKING 101 TIP

Weighing down the crust with pie weights or uncooked dried beans prevents the crust from bubbling up as it pre-bakes in the oven. If you use beans, save them for this purpose only since they can't be cooked afterward.

Bourbon-Pecan Tart with Chocolate Drizzle

1 cup packed brown sugar
¾ cup dark corn syrup
3 tablespoons all-purpose flour
2 tablespoons bourbon
2 tablespoons molasses
1 tablespoon butter, melted
½ teaspoon vanilla extract
¼ teaspoon salt
2 large eggs
1 large egg white
⅔ cup pecan halves
½ (14.1-ounce) package refrigerated pie dough
Cooking spray
½ ounce bittersweet chocolate, chopped

1. Preheat oven to 350°. Combine first 10 ingredients, stirring well with a whisk. Stir in pecans. Roll dough into a 13-inch circle on a lightly floured surface; fit into a 9-inch removable-bottom tart pan coated with cooking spray. Trim excess crust using a sharp knife. Spoon sugar mixture into prepared crust. Bake at 350° for 45 minutes or until center is set. Cool completely on a wire rack.
2. Place chocolate in a microwave-safe bowl; microwave at HIGH 1 minute. Stir until smooth. Drizzle chocolate evenly over tart. **Serves 12 (serving size: 1 wedge).**

CALORIES 277; FAT 10g (sat 2.7g, mono 3g, poly 1.5g); PROTEIN 2.4g; CARB 45.2g; FIBER 0.7g; CHOL 39mg; IRON 0.9mg; SODIUM 156mg; CALC 32mg

■ BAKING 101 TIP

Make the tart a day ahead, and store it in the refrigerator. You can use a 9-inch pie plate instead; simply roll the dough into a 13-inch circle, fold the edges under, and flute.

Blueberry-Peach Cobbler

5 pounds peaches, peeled, pitted, and sliced
2 tablespoons fresh lemon juice
1 cup granulated sugar, divided
⅜ teaspoon salt, divided
6.75 ounces (about 1½ cups) plus 2 tablespoons all-purpose flour, divided
Cooking spray
1 teaspoon baking powder
½ cup butter, softened
2 large eggs
1 teaspoon vanilla extract
¾ cup buttermilk
2 cups fresh blueberries
2 tablespoons turbinado sugar

1. Preheat oven to 375°. Place peaches in a large bowl. Drizzle with juice; toss. Add ¾ cup granulated sugar, ⅛ teaspoon salt, and 2 tablespoons flour to peach mixture; toss to combine. Spoon peach mixture into a 13 x 9–inch glass or ceramic baking dish coated with cooking spray.

2. Weigh or lightly spoon 6.75 ounces flour (about 1½ cups) into dry measuring cups; level with a knife. Combine 6.75 ounces flour, remaining ¼ teaspoon salt, and baking powder in a bowl, stirring well with a whisk. Place remaining ¼ cup granulated sugar and butter in a medium bowl, and beat with a mixer at medium speed until light and fluffy (about 2 minutes). Add eggs, 1 at a time, beating well after each addition. Stir in vanilla. Add flour mixture and buttermilk alternately to butter mixture, beginning and ending with flour mixture, beating just until combined. Fold in blueberries.

3. Spread batter evenly over peach mixture; sprinkle with turbinado sugar. Place baking dish on a foil-lined baking sheet. Bake at 375° for 1 hour or until topping is golden and filling is bubbly. **Serves 12 (serving size: about ¾ cup).**

CALORIES 303; FAT 9.6g (sat 5.4g, mono 2.4g, poly 0.7g); PROTEIN 5.1g; CARB 52.2g; FIBER 3.5g; CHOL 58mg; IRON 1.5mg; SODIUM 189mg; CALC 51mg

■ BAKING 101 TIP

Use peaches that aren't superripe for this recipe so they'll hold their shape when cooked. The baking dish will be brimming with fruit and topping, so it's a good idea to place it on a foil-lined baking sheet before putting it in the oven.

Fresh Cherry Cobbler

4 cups pitted fresh cherries (about 1¾ pounds)
1 cup sugar
3 tablespoons uncooked quick-cooking tapioca
1 tablespoon fresh lemon juice
⅛ teaspoon salt
½ (14.1-ounce) package refrigerated pie dough

1 large egg white, lightly beaten
1 tablespoon sugar
Cooking spray
2 tablespoons chilled butter, cut into small pieces

1. Preheat oven to 400°. Combine first 5 ingredients in a large bowl. Let stand 15 minutes.
2. While cherries stand, unroll dough and brush with egg white. Sprinkle with 1 tablespoon sugar. Cut dough into 8 (9 x 1–inch) strips. Cut dough strips crosswise into 1-inch pieces. Spoon cherry mixture into an 8-inch square glass or ceramic baking dish coated with cooking spray. Sprinkle dough squares and butter over cherry mixture. Bake at 400° for 15 minutes. Reduce oven temperature to 375°, and bake an additional 30 minutes or until hot and bubbly.
Serves 8.

CALORIES 312; FAT 10.4g (sat 4.9g, mono 3.3g, poly 1g); PROTEIN 2.3g; CARB 54g; FIBER 1.7g; CHOL 13mg; IRON 0.3mg; SODIUM 171mg; CALC 12mg

■ SHORTCUT TIP

A cherry pitter makes quick work of preparing the fresh cherries.

Mango-Macadamia Crisp

¼ cup granulated sugar

2 teaspoons cornstarch

4 cups chopped peeled ripe mango (about 4 pounds)

3 tablespoons fresh lime juice

2 teaspoons butter, melted

Cooking spray

1.5 ounces all-purpose flour (about ⅓ cup)

3 tablespoons granulated sugar

1½ teaspoons brown sugar

½ teaspoon ground ginger

3 tablespoons chilled butter, cut into small pieces

3 tablespoons chopped macadamia nuts

1. Preheat oven to 400°. Combine ¼ cup granulated sugar and cornstarch in a large bowl, stirring well with a whisk. Add mango, juice, and 2 teaspoons melted butter; toss gently to combine. Spoon mango mixture into an 8-inch square glass or ceramic baking dish coated with cooking spray.

2. Weigh or lightly spoon flour into a dry measuring cup; level with a knife. Combine flour and next 3 ingredients, stirring well. Cut in 3 tablespoons butter with a pastry blender or 2 knives until mixture resembles coarse meal. Stir in nuts. Sprinkle flour mixture evenly over mango mixture. Bake at 400° for 40 minutes or until browned. **Serves 8 (serving size: about ½ cup).**

CALORIES 238; FAT 8.1g (sat 3.1g, mono 4.2g, poly 0.3g); PROTEIN 1.7g; CARB 43.7g; FIBER 3.3g; CHOL 14mg; IRON 0.6mg; SODIUM 49mg; CALC 21mg

PIES, COBBLERS & CRUMBLES

prep
time:
20
minutes

■ SHORTCUT TIP

Mangoes have a large pit in the middle. To easily cut a mango, stand it upright, stem end up, and cut down lengthwise on each side of the pit. Score the flesh of each mango half into square cross-sections, slicing to but not through the skin. Turn the halves inside out and cut the chunks from the skin. Substitute bottled refrigerated mango for fresh if it's more convenient.

Homestead Pear Crisp

⅔ cup packed brown sugar, divided
2 tablespoons cornstarch
2 tablespoons fresh lemon juice
2 teaspoons ground cinnamon
¼ teaspoon salt
12 peeled Bartlett pears (about 5 pounds), cored and cut into ½-inch pieces

Cooking spray
2.25 ounces all-purpose flour (about ½ cup)
1 cup old-fashioned rolled oats
½ teaspoon ground cinnamon
6 tablespoons chilled butter, cut into small pieces

1. Preheat oven to 350°. Combine ⅓ cup brown sugar and next 5 ingredients in a large bowl; toss well. Spoon into a 13 x 9–inch glass or ceramic baking dish coated with cooking spray.
2. Weigh or lightly spoon flour into a dry measuring cup; level with a knife. Combine flour, oats, remaining ⅓ cup brown sugar, and cinnamon in a large bowl. Cut in butter with a pastry blender or 2 knives until mixture resembles coarse meal. Sprinkle flour mixture over pear mixture. Bake at 350° for 1 hour or until topping is golden and fruit is tender. Serve warm. **Serves 12 (serving size: about 1 cup).**

CALORIES 251; FAT 6.5g (sat 3.7g, mono 1.7g, poly 0.5g); PROTEIN 2.3g; CARB 49.2g; FIBER 6.7g; CHOL 15mg; IRON 1.4mg; SODIUM 96mg; CALC 43mg

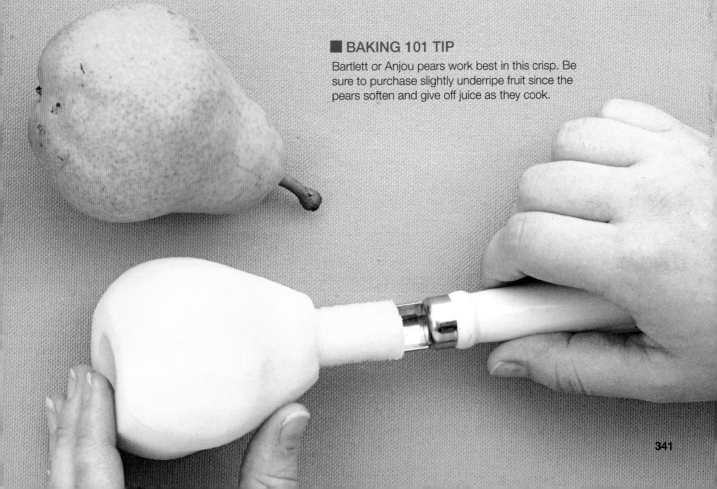

◾ BAKING 101 TIP

Bartlett or Anjou pears work best in this crisp. Be sure to purchase slightly underripe fruit since the pears soften and give off juice as they cook.

prep time: **15** minutes

Blackberry Crumble

10 cups fresh blackberries
⅓ cup granulated sugar
¼ cup cornstarch
1 tablespoon fresh lemon juice
Dash of salt
Cooking spray
4.5 ounces all-purpose flour (about 1 cup)

1 cup packed brown sugar
1 tablespoon finely chopped almonds, toasted
¼ teaspoon ground cinnamon
⅛ teaspoon salt
7 tablespoons chilled butter, cut into small pieces

1. Preheat oven to 400°. Combine first 5 ingredients in a large bowl, tossing well to coat. Spoon blackberry mixture into a 3-quart or 13 x 9–inch glass or ceramic baking dish coated with cooking spray.
2. Weigh or lightly spoon flour into a dry measuring cup; level with a knife. Combine flour and next 4 ingredients in a medium bowl; cut in butter with a pastry blender or 2 knives until mixture resembles coarse meal. Sprinkle flour mixture over blackberry mixture. Bake at 400° for 35 minutes or until filling is thick and bubbly and topping is browned. Remove from oven; let stand 20 minutes. Serve warm. **Serves 10 (serving size: about ⅔ cup).**

CALORIES 306; FAT 9.3g (sat 5.2g, mono 2.4g, poly 0.8g); PROTEIN 3.6g; CARB 55.2g; FIBER 7.7g; CHOL 21mg; IRON 1.7mg; SODIUM 109mg; CALC 67mg

■ BAKING 101 TIP
Adding cornstarch to the blackberry mixture helps thicken it, creating a sweet, syrupy filling. If you have very juicy berries, you may need to increase the cornstarch.

Santa Rosa Plum Crumble

14 plums, each cut into 6 wedges
¼ cup granulated sugar
3 tablespoons dry red wine
1 (4-inch) piece vanilla bean, split lengthwise
Cooking spray
3.4 ounces all-purpose flour (about ¾ cup)
1 cup old-fashioned rolled oats

6 tablespoons brown sugar
1½ teaspoons grated orange rind
¼ teaspoon salt
⅛ teaspoon ground nutmeg
5 tablespoons chilled butter, cut into small pieces

1. Preheat oven to 375°. Combine first 3 ingredients in a large bowl. Scrape seeds from vanilla bean; add seeds to plum mixture. Discard bean. Toss mixture gently to combine. Spoon into a 13 x 9–inch glass or ceramic baking dish coated with cooking spray.

2. Weigh or lightly spoon flour into dry measuring cups; level with a knife. Combine flour and next 5 ingredients in a medium bowl; cut in butter with a pastry blender or 2 knives until mixture resembles coarse meal. Sprinkle flour mixture evenly over plum mixture. Bake at 375° for 45 minutes or until plum mixture is bubbly and topping is lightly browned. **Serves 9 (serving size: about 1 cup).**

CALORIES 284; FAT 8.2g (sat 4.1g, mono 2.8g, poly 0.7g); PROTEIN 3.8g; CARB 52.5g; FIBER 3.9g; CHOL 17mg; IRON 1.3mg; SODIUM 134mg; CALC 24mg

■ BAKING 101 TIP
Santa Rosa plums are great in this dessert, although any juicy plum will work nicely. This crumble is good served either warm or at room temperature, so it's an ideal make-ahead dessert.

prep time: **15** minutes

Baking Substitution Guide

If you're right in the middle of cooking and realize you don't have
a particular ingredient, refer to the substitutions in this list.

INGREDIENT	SUBSTITUTION
Baking Products	
Baking powder, 1 teaspoon	½ teaspoon cream of tartar and ¼ teaspoon baking soda
Chocolate	
Semisweet, 1 ounce	1 ounce unsweetened chocolate and 1 tablespoon sugar
Unsweetened, 1 ounce	3 tablespoons cocoa and 1 tablespoon butter or margarine
Cocoa, ¼ cup	1 ounce unsweetened chocolate (decrease fat in recipe by ½ tablespoon)
Coconut, fresh, grated, 1½ tablespoons	1 tablespoon flaked coconut
Cornstarch, 1 tablespoon	2 tablespoons all-purpose flour or granular tapioca
Flour	
All-purpose, 1 tablespoon	1½ teaspoons cornstarch, potato starch, or rice starch
Cake, 1 cup sifted	1 cup minus 2 tablespoons all-purpose flour
Self-rising, 1 cup	1 cup all-purpose flour, 1 teaspoon baking powder, and ½ teaspoon salt
Sugar, powdered, 1 cup	1 cup sugar and 1 tablespoon cornstarch (processed in food processor)
Honey, ½ cup	½ cup molasses or maple syrup
Eggs	
1 large	2 egg yolks for custards and cream fillings or 2 egg yolks and 1 tablespoon water for cookies
1 large	¼ cup egg substitute
2 large	3 small eggs
1 egg white (2 tablespoons)	2 tablespoons egg substitute
1 egg yolk (1½ tablespoons)	2 tablespoons sifted dry egg yolk powder and 2 teaspoons water or 1½ tablespoons thawed frozen egg yolk
Dairy Products	
Milk	
Buttermilk, low-fat or nonfat, 1 cup	1 tablespoon lemon juice or vinegar and 1 cup low-fat or fat-free milk (let stand 10 minutes)
Fat-free milk, 1 cup	4 to 5 tablespoons fat-free dry milk powder; enough cold water to make 1 cup
Sour cream, 1 cup	1 cup plain yogurt
Seasonings	
Garlic, 1 clove	1 teaspoon bottled minced garlic
Ginger	
Crystallized, 1 tablespoon	⅛ teaspoon ground ginger
Fresh, grated, 1 tablespoon	⅛ teaspoon ground ginger
Herbs, fresh, 1 tablespoon	1 teaspoon dried herbs or ¼ teaspoon ground herbs (except rosemary)
Vanilla bean, 6-inch bean	1 tablespoon vanilla extract

Nutritional Analysis

What the Numbers Mean For You

To interpret the nutritional analysis in *Cooking Light Everyday Baking*, use the figures below as a daily reference guide. One size doesn't fit all, so take lifestyle, age, and circumstances into consideration. For example, pregnant or breast-feeding women need more protein, calories, and calcium. Go to choosemyplate.gov for your own individualized plan.

We Use These Abbreviations in Our Nutritional Analysis

sat	saturated fat	**CHOL**	cholesterol
mono	monounsaturated fat	**CALC**	calcium
poly	polyunsaturated fat	**g**	gram
CARB	carbohydrates	**mg**	milligram

Daily Nutrition Guide

	Women ages 25 to 50	Women over 50	Men ages 25 to 50	Men over 50
Calories	2,000	2,000*	2,700	2,500
Protein	50g	50g	63g	60g
Fat	65g*	65g*	88g*	83g*
Saturated Fat	20g*	20g*	27g*	25g*
Carbohydrates	304g	304g	410g	375g
Fiber	25g to 35g	25g to 35g	25g to 35g	25g to 35g
Cholesterol	300mg*	300mg*	300mg*	300mg*
Iron	18mg	8mg	8mg	8mg
Sodium	2,300mg*	1,500mg*	2,300mg*	1,500mg*
Calcium	1,000mg	1,200mg	1,000mg	1,000 mg

* Or less, for optimum health

Nutritional values used in our calculations either come from the food processor, version 10.4 (ESHA research), or are provided by food manufacturers.

Metric Equivalents

The information in the following charts is provided to help cooks outside the United States successfully use the recipes in this book. All equivalents are approximate.

Cooking/Oven Temperatures

	Fahrenheit	Celsius	Gas Mark
Freeze Water	32° F	0° C	
Room Temp.	68° F	20° C	
Boil Water	212° F	100° C	
Bake	325° F	160° C	3
	350° F	180° C	4
	375° F	190° C	5
	400° F	200° C	6
	425° F	220° C	7
	450° F	230° C	8
Broil			Grill

Liquid Ingredients by Volume

¼ tsp	=	1 ml				
½ tsp	=	2 ml				
1 tsp	=	5 ml				
3 tsp	=	1 tbl	=	½ fl oz	=	15 ml
2 tbls	=	⅛ cup	=	1 fl oz	=	30 ml
4 tbls	=	¼ cup	=	2 fl oz	=	60 ml
5⅓ tbls	=	⅓ cup	=	3 fl oz	=	80 ml
8 tbls	=	½ cup	=	4 fl oz	=	120 ml
10⅔ tbls	=	⅔ cup	=	5 fl oz	=	160 ml
12 tbls	=	¾ cup	=	6 fl oz	=	180 ml
16 tbls	=	1 cup	=	8 fl oz	=	240 ml
1 pt	=	2 cups	=	16 fl oz	=	480 ml
1 qt	=	4 cups	=	32 fl oz	=	960 ml
				33 fl oz	=	1000 ml = 1l

Dry Ingredients by Weight

(To convert ounces to grams, multiply the number of ounces by 30.)

1 oz	=	¹⁄₁₆ lb	=	30 g
4 oz	=	¼ lb	=	120 g
8 oz	=	½ lb	=	240 g
12 oz	=	¾ lb	=	360 g
16 oz	=	1 lb	=	480 g

Length

(To convert inches to centimeters, multiply the number of inches by 2.5.)

1 in	=			2.5 cm	
6 in	=	½ ft	=	15 cm	
12 in	=	1 ft	=	30 cm	
36 in	=	3 ft	= 1 yd =	90 cm	
40 in	=			100 cm	= 1m

Equivalents for Different Types of Ingredients

Standard Cup	Fine Powder (ex. flour)	Grain (ex. rice)	Granular (ex. sugar)	Liquid Solids (ex. butter)	Liquid (ex. milk)
1	140 g	150 g	190 g	200 g	240 ml
¾	105 g	113 g	143 g	150 g	180 ml
⅔	93 g	100 g	125 g	133 g	160 ml
½	70 g	75 g	95 g	100 g	120 ml
⅓	47 g	50 g	63 g	67 g	80 ml
¼	35 g	38 g	48 g	50 g	60 ml
⅛	18 g	19 g	24 g	25 g	30 ml

index

INDEX